THE GREAT FUTURE
OF
AMERICA & AFRICA.

THE GREAT FUTURE
OF
AMERICA AND AFRICA

BY
JACOB DEWEES

The Black Heritage Library Collection

79-1081

BOOKS FOR LIBRARIES PRESS
FREEPORT, NEW YORK
1971

First Published 1854
Reprinted 1971

N
E448
D S
1971
c. 2

Reprinted from a copy in the
Fisk University Library Negro Collection

INTERNATIONAL STANDARD BOOK NUMBER:
0-8369-8786-1

LIBRARY OF CONGRESS CATALOG CARD NUMBER:
75-154075

PRINTED IN THE UNITED STATES OF AMERICA

THE GREAT FUTURE

OF

AMERICA AND AFRICA;

AN ESSAY SHOWING

Our Whole Duty to the Black Man,

CONSISTENT WITH

Our Own Safety and Glory.

BY JACOB DEWEES, M. D.

"The charges against me are all of one kind; that I have pushed the principles of general justice and benevolence too far—farther than a cautious policy would warrant; and farther than the opinions of many would go along with me,.—In every accident which may happen through life,—I will call to mind this accusation and be comforted!"—BURKE.

PHILADELPHIA.
PRINTED FOR THE AUTHOR BY H. ORR,
No. 100 Chestnut St.
1854.

Entered according to Act of Congress, in the year 1854, by Jacob Dewees, M. D. in the Office of the Clerk of the District Court, in and for the Eastern District of Pennsylvania.

CONTENTS.

CHAPTER I.—Slavery a Disease.

Where shall we find a Remedy? ... 17
The Two Doctors. Dr. Colonization's Treatment ... 20
Dr Abolition's Treatment ... 26
Justice to the Master demands a Combined Practice ... 30

CHAPTER II.—Slavery, if perpetuated, fatal to Nations.

Teachings of the Egyptian Bondage of Israel, its divine Purpose ... 35
Parallel between Egyptian and American Bondage ... 38
Reason calls for the Exodus of the African Race ... 40
What duties—what sacrifices the call demands of us ... 43
What the Past says to the Future, if we refuse the Demand ... 45
The inevitable Fate of Nations—how shall we retard it? ... 46
The *consent* of all parties necessary to the Exodus ... 48

CHAPTER III.—The Public Domain viewed as a Means for Emancipation.

Degrading Effects of the Mismanagement and Misappropriation of the Domain ... 50
Description, History, and Extent of the Domain ... 56
Abuses and Proper Uses of the Domain ... 60
Congress unfit to manage the Domain ... 68

CHAPTER IV.—Plan for Constitutionally Removing the Public Lands from the Custody of Congress, and for effecting Emancipation.

Proposal for a Convention of the People to consider the Subjects of Emancipation, Colonization, and the Appropriation of the Public Domain ... 71
Plan of Organization for a Board of the Public Domain ... 72
Appropriations to Public Works in Africa, to prepare for the Exodus ... 73
Education of the Young Negro for Usefulness in Africa ... 75
The "Redemption" System will aid the Exodus ... 76
Immense Results of the Plan, in Civilizing and Christianizing Africa ... 77
Proposed Appropriations for American Public Schools, which would ultimately extinguish the State Debts, &c ... 79
Folly of the "Free Homestead." Scheme when contrasted with this Plan ... 80

viii   CONTENTS.

Means of preventing Injury to the South from the loss of Slave Laborers during the Exodus, by encouraging American Manufactures............. 80
Necessity of prudently husbanding the Proceeds of the Domain, to remunerate the Master for the loss of the Slave... 81
Amplitude of our Resources to meet all Demands, if carefully managed............................ 82
Beneficial Results of the proposed Management of the Domain upon Agriculture, Commerce, Currency, and Public Morals............................... 84
Tendency of California Gold to extend Slave Territory.......... 91
Farther Remarks on the Evil Tendency of the Free Homestead Bill......................... 93

CHAPTER V.—First Duties of the proposed Board of the Public Domain, in relation to the Exodus.

Preparation of Africa for the Reception of Immigrants...... 96
Preparation of Colored Artizans and Teachers of Religion, for Emigration to Africa....... 97
Adaptation of African Rivers for public Improvements....... 100
Relation of the River Niger to Liberia and the Nile............ ib.
Vast field for Rail-roads and Internal Trade........................ 101
Grandeur of the Future of Africa, if aided according to the proposed Plan..................... 105
The Execution of the Plan would pay in full our Debt to the Negro Race 107

CHAPTER VI.—Our Tendency to National Decay through the Influence of Slavery, proved by the Earlier and more Recent History of our policy.

Active Interest of the People in the policy of Government, in Colonial Times.................... 110
The same Activity in Early National Times...................... 117
The Administration of John Adams. 118
Acquisition of Right of Entry on Indian Lands by Treaty.. ib.
Popular Resistance against Law, how met........................... 119
The Administration of Thomas Jefferson........................... 121
Weakness of the Frontier....... ib.
Weakness of the Government.... ib.
The Administration of James Madison............................. 122
War with England............... ib.
Project for demanding Canada as an Indemnity.................. 123
This Action discountenanced by Government...................... ib.
Apathy of the Federalists and general calm, but Honesty in management of Affairs......... 124
The Administration of James Monroe.............................. 125
Just Guardianship of the Public Lands............................. ib.
Early but trifling pre-emption Grants............................ 125
Prudence and Economy still predominant. .... ib.
First comsiderable Grants of Land for Public Improvements 128
The St. Joseph's Purchase....... ib.
The Administration of Andrew Jackson. 129
Reverse of the Picture............ ib.
Large Purchase of Land from the Indians....................... ib.
Loose extensions of the Right of Pre-emption...................... 130
Attempts to check mad Speculations in Lands.................. 132
Financial Ignorance................ ib.
Agricultural madness and its consequences 133

CONTENTS.

Apparent Prosperity.................. ib.
Causes of the consequent Collapse 134
Retirement of Andrew Jackson.. ib.
Administration of Martin Van Buren—he "treads in the footsteps,"........................ 135
Financial Crisis..................... ib.
Suspension of Specie Payments. 136
False Views and False Policy.. 137
Administration of William Henry Harrison, and John Tyler................................ 139
No Wisdom learned from Experience. 140
Extravagance, Corruption, and abuse of the Public Domain continued. .... ib.
Administration of Jas. K. Polk.. 141
The Mexican War, for the extension of Slavery, and Speculation in State Debt.......... ib.
No Reformation of Abuses....... 143
Presidential Usurpation........... 144
Proposal to reduce the Price of certain unsold Lands to Twenty Five Cents per Acre.. 145
Millions of Acres Squandered... 146
Administration of Zachary Taylor and Millard Fillmore....... 152
Application of California for Admission into the Union..... ib.
The Slave Question in full Agitation .... ib.
Efforts to dissolve the Union... ib.
The Compromise.................... ib.
Administration of Franklin Pierce 153
The Pre-emption Laws at the Bottom of the disasters of the Country. 154
The Free Homestead Bill, the longest step in the march of National Decay................... ib.
The Inevitable consequences of our present Policy, in relation to Territory, if continued in connexion with the Permanence of Slavery......... 156

CHAPTER VII.—A plain talk with the Free Man of Colour in the United States.

Motives for an African Exodus.. 168
The Influence of the Abolitionist injurious to the Slave..... 169
Kindness the Law, and Cruelty the exception with the Slave Master: but the Exceptions are such that Humanity demands Emancipation........... 170
The Establishment of an African Nationality essential to the Advancement of Freeman and Slave......................... ib.
The Abolitionists substitute Feeling for Reason, in Argument and Practice; they act upon Individual cases illegally, and advocate the Impracticable............................ 172
Equality impossible to the Free Coloured Man here----Consequences of attempting it....... 173
America has nothing to offer the Free Coloured Man here, comparable with African Independence....................... 174
Political Objects of the Abolitionist Agitators.................. ib.
The Attempt at unconditional Emancipation must produce Civil War........................ 175
Condition of the African Race in Civil War..................... 176
Possibility of a peaceful Division of the Union Condition of the Coloured Race in that Case.... 177
Twe distinct Races cannot exist together in Equality............ 178
The true political Position of the African Race in this Country. 179
The Coloured American still a Captive African.................. 180
Rights of Captives................ ib.
Value of the plea of Necessity in excusing the forced Retention of a Captive. 181
Peculiarities of African Capti-

vity, and their political Consequences... 181

Reasons why the Free Man of Colour should favour Colonization and African Nationality... 184

Reasons for Exodus, though all Public aid should be refused.. 186

Climate of Africa; folly of judging it by the health of the Coast... 187

African health and difficulties compared with those of our early Colonies, &c... 191

Effects of African Progress on Slavery in the United States.. ib.

Folly of depending upon the pretended political friends of the Negro, for political elevation here... 194

False friendship of Great Britain. 195

Folly of depending upon Nations or People for aid, "because it is right."... 197

Is there "labor enough for all" in this Country?... 211

Proposed exploration of Africa by Free Blacks... 215

Further remarks on the erroneous Policy of the Abolitionists... 220

Concluding Appeals... 222

TO THE CONGRESS OF THE UNITED STATES.

In recommending this Essay to your serious attention, I am actuated by no disrespectful motive, though approaching you with the self-confidence of a legitimate American sovereign, addressing the no less legitimate agents of the sovereign authority.

That our Union has been, and still is endangered by the great sectional question of the age, *you know*—that the embarrassments of that question have been increased by a fatal policy in relation to that heaviest of national trusts, the Public Domain, *I believe:*—therefore, as a party directly interested in that trust, and familiar with its history, I feel bound, in justice to myself, my country, and the heirs of her greatness, to object to the manner in which it has been administered by you. The grounds of my objections, and my idea of the mode in which the trust may be made conducive to our national glory and prosperity, to the removal of the greatest evil which threatens our future, and to the present and permanent happiness of more races than one—are developed in the following pages, which to you are hereby
Respectfully dedicated
By your constituent and fellow citizen,
THE AUTHOR.

Upper Merion, Montgomery County, Pa., May, 1854.

PREFACE.

The following pages are addressed alike to the American of the white race, and the free Negro of the United States. They embrace the outline of an extensive system of reform, including the ultimate emancipation of the entire African race; not by the slow process of colonization, by a private society with slender means; nor by the headlong policy of "abolition," which asks of the master sacrifices that never will be—never can be made. This system includes also the permanent and effectual establishment of common schools, with ample provision for their maintenance; and it provides incidentally for the gradual extinguishment of the debts of those states which are now burdened with such responsibilities, and for many other public facilities to all the states, without undue or inequitable advantage to any of them. Nor, in effecting these desirable purposes, does it propose any unconstitutional or anti-American proceeding.

The reader will be startled, perhaps, at the vastness of such a scheme. Probably, he may exclaim, "where shall we find the means for such an incalculably expensive project?" The author is liable to all the errors inseparable from human judgment —he may be liable to the misleadings of enthusiasm; but—*read and decide!* He cannot plead ignorance of the problem which he has undertaken to discuss, in excuse for his mistakes; for, he has not attempted to wander beyond the field in which he has grown gray in observation and reflection. Unless, then, he has been strangely deceived by his wishes, the reader will rise from the perusal of these pages, convinced that our beloved country holds at her command wealth amply sufficient to accomplish all these ends, as rapidly as their accomplishment is desirable,—and this without jarring the finances, or imposing fresh burdens on the public. Nay more! He sincerely believes that the system of appropriation herein recommended supplies the only hope of checking the current of public corruption, and also much of the private and petty looseness of morals by which both government and society have been advanced in degradation within the last twenty years.

The mere attempt to secure such blessings for his fellow citizens, requires no apology from the author; he feels that it, also, confers upon him the right to expect a careful examination of his views, *before even they are condemned*—and he asks no more.

To the free man of color he would say, that, in the final chapter, which is especially addressed to him, there will be found no flattery, but ample kindness. It is very rarely that persons of this class receive direct attention from those who discuss their interests and their well-being. It may be invidious to attribute this fact to the real indifference of pretended friendship, where nothing is to be gained personally by the seeming philanthropist; but, the fear of hostility should not lead us to the concealment of truth. In the picture of the hopelessness of the political condition of the African race with us, and the bright future of Africa, this treatise offers to that race the only advice that can prove truly and practically useful to it; and the author has no hesitation in urging the genuine philanthropist to press the consideration of this advice upon the down-trodden people who wear

"The shadowed livery of the burnished sun,"

OUR WHOLE DUTY TO THE BLACK MAN.

CHAPTER I.

SLAVERY A DISEASE.

Allegorical Account of the past Treatment of Slavery — Its Treatment by the Colonizationists, and by the Abolitionists — Both have neglected the Magnitude of the Evil, and the Question of Justice to the Master in the Remedy — A combined Treatment necessary.

WHAT is to be done with Slavery in the United States? This is a question which urges itself upon every inquiring and reflecting mind, when we observe, for the last few years, with the assembling of each Congress, the whole nation convulsed in contending on the one hand for, and on the other against, some new principle applicable to Slavery. Moreover, the mind of individuals, of nations, and indeed of the whole Christian community is aroused, and full of inquiry into the subject of African Slavery, especially as it exists in the United States.

This inquiry, in itself, naturally suggests the question, why is it that Slavery, especially chattel slavery, exists at all? The causes are numerous, but the most prominent of those which have led to its establishment in the United States are, the love of power which one nation desires to exercise over another, with a view to wealth regardless of the means, and a licentious indulgence of human passions, to secure national wealth and individual idleness.

In each and every cause conducing to chattel slavery and its continuance, you will find concealed the germ of an evil, which, in its full development, destroys the glory of nations. But these causes have been so thoroughly examined, and are so fully understood, that little remains to be said upon the subject; nor do I desire to do so. *My* object is, to point out the mode of practically adapting *means* to the accomplishment of emancipation in the United States. With this view, I shall be obliged to speak, first, of what has been done; and secondly, what yet remains to be done, whenever it shall become the desire of the nation to render justice to the African. And when speaking of what ought to be done in order that the means may be made sufficient to the purposed end, I feel I am treading upon the borders of a field which has not yet been cultivated by the people with sufficient zeal and care to produce a profitable harvest; a field upon which so few of the advocates of African emancipation have entered, in order to show the world its length and breadth, its resources, its fertility of soil and its capacity of being cultivated, that I fear I shall be traversing a country little known, its value little understood, and, perhaps, little cared for, though capable of contributing immensely to the advantage of both master and slave. To the development of the vast promise of this region my efforts shall be directed.

Nearly all that has yet been attempted with a view to the entire emancipation of slaves in the United States, has been done by the "Colonization" and "Abolition" societies; the one society looking forward to the time when, through its means, ultimate emancipation shall be consummated—the other, claiming to emancipate at once and unconditionally, upon the abstract principle of *right to the slave*. If this latter Society would include *justice to the master* in its theories, then, in point of feeling, little difference would exist between them.

But whatever may be the opinions, sentiments, and rules of conduct on the part of these societies, all thinking men admit that slavery, as it exists amongst us, is a disease of the most fearful character, in its consequences upon the body politic; that it is an excrescence of vast magnitude, tending to react upon, and debilitate the whole body in such a way as to produce an unhealthy action throughout the entire system. The symptoms of the disease which this excrescence has already produced, are not to be mistaken; they are of a *convulsive* character. The excrescence has taken deep root, and is of long standing; and although measures to check the further growth of the tumour have been in part successful, the many attempts which have been made to destroy it seem never to have had the desired effect, but, on the contrary, whenever a cure has been talked of and attempted, the symptoms have invariably tended towards "convulsion."

To cure this evil, two physicians presented themselves. Both have tried their skill, and neither has yet given up the patient.

The first, recommended that such remedies should be applied as would cause portions of the protuberance to drop off, from time to time, and create as little irritability in the nerves of the patient as possible; and the employment of means promising such results met the approbation of many of the best friends of the patient. The remedies, too, seemed to be such as common sense and correct reasoning would dictate; but the cure has not been effected by these means. Yet many, very many of the most ardent admirers of the sufferer, won even to an untiring attachment by his solid virtues, still believe that the removing of the excrescence by mild remedies, such as tend gradually to reduce the size of the protuberance, without the loss of blood or a violent agitation of the system, constitutes the only proper plan of cure. They are, moreover, fully possessed of the belief that, if something effective is not speedily done to eradicate the tumour and allay the irritability of the patient, his constitution will be fatally undermined at no distant day. This doctor has the fullest confidence that his remedies, given in doses large enough to produce the desired effect, would complete the cure; but he complains that the medicine is of the most costly character; that, thus far, he has been at the entire expense of providing it; that he has borne this expense in consequence of his regard and high respect for the patient, and that he could desire nothing more than that he should enjoy a long life and happy old age. But, for all this, the patient does not look smilingly on the means of cure. He will not even acknowledge that one of the remedies upon which the doctor piques himself very much, as having been the means of great relief, is really a good remedy; being fearful, perhaps, that if he should acknowledge its excellent and beneficial influence, he would be called upon to purchase largely of the costly article. Now in this, I think Uncle Samuel — I may as well name him, for no doubt you, reader, have a great regard for him — behaves much like the miser who would rather suffer a consuming disease to prey upon his very vitals, than be at the expense of a dose of medicine, but never fails to swallow such medicines as are supplied gratuitously by his friends.

But this manifestation on the part of the old gentleman is somewhat strange; for he is rich, and can hardly be said to be miserly, as he spends money in vast sums for all necessary purposes. Indeed, in anything that seems to improve his condition, he never appears backward. He has one very bad fault, however, which is, that in all that relates to his health or the management of his estate, he has a too willing ear for the quack in medicine and the demagogue in politics; consequently he is often the victim of deceit in his undertakings. For example; not very long ago, he was persuaded that one of his neighbours had a very valuable farm adjoining his own; that he ought to purchase it, and that he could do so to the great advantage of his whole family, especially as his neighbour owed him a considerable sum of money. But it so turned out that his neighbour was not very willing to sell. He was then advised to give him a few kicks and cuffs, and threaten to drive him off his farm altogether; upon which no doubt he would be able to purchase.

Well, he followed this advice. He broke the peace, and gave his neighbour a most awful drubbing. This drubbing cost him a round sum of money. He had also to buy the land at full price afterwards; yet, and as soon as the purchase was made, these same persons who persuaded him to do a thing not calculated to elevate his character for noble deeds, turned right upon him, and advised him to *give away* all the lands thus purchased, and all such besides as might be in his possession and unoccupied, in other places, in parcels of one hundred and sixty acres, to any and everybody who might choose to take them as a gift, whether such persons should have contributed much, or little, or nothing, to the acquisition of these lands! The good that would result from this advice was not easily to be understood — the evil connected with it seemed palpable. That such a measure should be expected to result in good, seemed to be in direct opposition to all the dictates of political economy, and in violation of all experience in the management of individual estates. That such a measure would incapacitate the old gentleman from carrying forward to a successful issue any large project of philanthropy, in relation to education or anything else, in improving his estate by new roads, or, indeed, in effecting improvements of any kind — scarcely admits of a doubt.

That a like policy would ruin an individual, and render every member of his family beggars, is most certain. Uncle Samuel understood, too, that wherever land ranged at the highest prices, *there* was the the most industry observable, and *there* was the enjoyment of the most liberal distribution of comforts. So he could not be persuaded to give away his lands. But unfortunately, just at this time, it was discovered that his new purchase contained a vast amount of gold! And then, without asking Uncle Samuel, " Will you give me the land or not ?" away these people ran from all parts of the world, China and all, and, taking the land without money and without price, began to dig gold. Now the worst feature in all this lawlessness is, that when the old gentleman sent his strong men to whip his neighbour into selling part of his farm, he absolutely weakened himself, both morally and physically, so much, that he was powerless in defence of his own property ! Had he made an honourable purchase, he could have controlled his property by the same force with which he subdued his neighbour; by which means he could have maintained his lawful authority and his just rights.

Here we find a source of the deepest regret. Under this depredation upon his rights, he loses, first, all claim to high moral conduct, and, secondly, he also loses the very means required to purchase the expensive remedy already referred to, without which his life will probably be sacrificed; which means might be abundantly procured from his newly-purchased acres.

Leaving our allegory for the moment, it is plain that a reasonable rent for the California gold mines would secure a revenue that would colonize every African in the United States in the course of one hundred years. Nor ought the entire emancipation of the slave to be consummated in less time, if we would give to him the largest advantages which emancipation is capable of rendering him.

But, (to resume our parable,) when Uncle Samuel has shown himself on the one hand entirely regardless of the means of cure applicable to his case, and, on the other, has displayed an utter recklessness of conduct by not refraining from such practices as are calculated to spread the disease more widely, how can we believe that he is sincere in his avowed fears that the disease will prove fatal to him in mind and body? Yet it is certain, and he knows it as well as any one, that this disease never yet failed to destroy those upon whom it laid its festering fangs, body and soul! It has been seen, too, that the old gentleman has a hankering after the estates of his neighbours, and as he grows more prodigal in his expenses *and immoral in his practices,* he seems to entertain less fear of the disease than he did in his youth, and still refuses to spend money in medicine; so that the first doctor is quite out of patience as well as purse.

Another set of friends, who advocate a different medical school, being determined that he should not die by obstinacy, forced upon him the attendance of another physician, who called himself Abolition, and who loved Uncle Samuel as much as did Colonization; but he was more ardent in his feelings, and pronounced the continuance of the disease death to the patient, and said that the longer it continued, the more difficult would be the cure; that everything that had been done thus far had been of no use; that the disease was daily growing worse; that even the remedies which he once thought were calculated to do good, he was now convinced were all pernicious in character, and oppressive and demoralizing in effect. With the same confident boldness, he asserted that the disease was gangrenous, and that nothing short of immediate extirpation would save the patient's life.

To this course of practice the old gentleman demurred. He was fearful that the removing of the disease at one single operation would kill him; and, in this opinion, he had some of his best tried friends to agree with him. He gave, as further reasons why the operation should not be performed, that he had inherited the disease; that it had now become *constitutional* with him; that although he should submit to the operation of having the gangrenous part of the excrescence removed, he was fearful the disease would break out in sores upon other parts of the body, and that the remedy proposed, would, after all, prove to be ineffectual. The doctor then contended that, if extirpation was not allowed, it would be absolutely necessary to use such means as would tend to prevent the disease from spreading, and that it often happened, especially in diseases of the *skin*, that the application of a blister plaster upon parts of the body where the skin was yet sound, but predisposed to the disease, would prevent the malady from extending itself over the whole body. This remedy, he thought would, in all probability, also prevent this gangrenous sore, although deep-rooted, from enlarging itself in its malignant proportions. At all events, he declared that there could be no very serious harm in trying it; for that, in the youth of the patient, this disease showed itself with all its malignant symptoms in *dark spots* over the whole body, and, in consequence, a large plaster was applied over more than one-half the surface, black spots and all. By this application, he said, the disease was prevented from extending itself over the parts to which the remedy was applied; yet he was sorry to acknowledge that this remedy did not effect a complete cure, and bring ease and comfort to the black spots; that, in them, the evils of the disease still continued, and that the pains and sufferings which those spots still manifest, are such that even the parts where "the blister drew," cannot be said to be entirely healed. But, as the sore had become gangrenous upon those portions of the body to which the application had never been made, he held it right and proper to employ it there, in order to prevent the disease from spreading over parts where the skin had always been sound. But being not exactly clear in his own mind that the remedy he proposed would have the desired effect, he candidly stated that only a few years before his brother Colonization took charge of the case, a remedy similar to the one he was now proposing had been again tried; but the blister was not fairly drawn before the symptoms of *convulsion* in the patient grew so strong, that a large portion of the plaster was cut off, and it was not allowed to extend beyond a certain line upon the body. This had the effect of allaying the irritability of the patient. Yet that the remedy was a good one, he had not the least doubt; for, so far as the plaster was allowed to take effect, there was no appearance of these black spots in a malignant form; and rather than not try the remedy, he would apply it if he was sure that it would convulse the whole body of the patient, even to dissolution! He made the application, and it had the effect of producing convulsions throughout the whole system; so much so, that fears began to be entertained upon all sides, that the *constitution* of Uncle Samuel would give way under the operation. The doctor was then compelled to yield to the solicitations of many of the old gentleman's old advisers — who were men that believed he had a constitution so strong and so well balanced for the attainment of good health, that it would naturally throw off, in time, the scrofulous disease inherited from his ancestors. The doctor had to submit to the compromise. But he did not do it gracefully, or with a good will. He still says that he cannot be mistaken in the prognostics of the disease, and that he will continue from time to time to apply the proper remedy, although the patient should die under the operation. Thus far, however, his efforts seem to tend towards an aggravation of the disease upon those parts of the body where the sore is most deeply rooted. This sore has in many instances assumed a most inflammatory character; it has become more painful in itself; it festers, and throws off a vast quantity of frothy matter; it requires more bandaging to keep it within its old limits. Even the pressure of the bandages aggravate the disease. It cannot be said that the abolition doctor has accomplished much by the application of any of his remedies. Yet I think it must be allowed that he has effected much more by his assiduous inquiries into the nature of the disease, and that he is not unreasonable in his opinion, that the death of the patient is inevitable if the disease be not cured. He has brought all right-minded men to a full conviction that he is correct in his *prognostics*, though he is wrong in his *remedies!*

The theory that aims at the true means of emancipation in the United States, must *combine justice to the master* with *freedom to the slave.* Such is the decided conclusion of men who have not as yet actively espoused the opinion of either of these doctors, for the reason that the one does not aim directly at emancipation, and that the other denies justice to the master. A combination of the views of these two societies might be made to place in our possession vastly more efficient means for carrying out the great work of redeeming from bondage the African in the United States. Many staunch friends of the country sincerely desire to see it healed of all gangrenous sores; and if they could, by imparting of their own means, effect a perfect cure, they would do so.

Although the Government displays a strange miserliness in not aiding so desirable a purpose, yet it will squander upon objects of little worth oceans of wealth, which, if applied in the right direction, would effectually secure the nation from the perpetuation of the terrible curse of slavery, and thus insure peace, safety, and prosperity at home, and honour and high distinction abroad.

The country is full of patriotic and enlightened men, who do not hesitate liberally to apply their private means to any grave purpose of national importance. With them must be classed a large proportion of the prominent and active members of both the Colonization and the Abolition societies, who, undiscouraged by the coldness of the Government and the passions of the sections, still labour with equal energy to rid the United States of the most threatening embarrassment to its march of unexampled prosperity, and (as I am bound to believe,) with equal honesty of purpose. But unfortunately, instead of uniting their energies in one common effort with each other, and with those of their fellow citizens who feel, and would make any sacrifice to remove this curse — instead of bringing their combined influence to bear upon the national authorities, in order to arouse them to their duties, these societies have been unhappily placed in antagonistic positions. The solution of the vexed problem of African slavery in America lies with neither the one, nor the other. It demands a union of the principles of both, and a conjoint effort between them, the people, and the rulers. This, and this only, can give a rational hope that the plague spots may be removed from the bosom of the country — that justice may be rendered alike to master and slave, to the white race and the black — that the future Africa may look back to the sufferings of her children in this land of liberty as a blessing, and to American Slavery as the mother of African Liberty and Civilization!

Such I believe to be the only practical mode for the accomplishment of a purpose fraught with the most magnificent consequences to the national glory and honour; and, to develop the plan, and point out the proper direction of this joint effort, is the purpose which I have humbly, but hopefully undertaken in the production of these pages.

CHAPTER II.

SLAVERY, IF PERPETUATED, FATAL TO A NATION.

The Divine intention of Slavery — Parallel between Egyptian and American bondage — Reason demands the Exodus of the African Race — What the Past says to the Future, if we refuse the Demand — How we may retard the inevitable fate of Nations — The consent of all parties interested necessary to the Exodus.

THAT it is the object of Colonization to elevate the free negro to a social standing, where he can appreciate and enjoy the blessings of freedom, I think cannot readily be denied; nor will any one have a doubt of the humanity of the scheme. Yet no one has presented or proposed a plan which shall embrace the means necessary to secure the political and social freedom of the slave, and which shall promise a definite period of time, however remote, when emancipation in the United States shall be consummated upon the broadest base of charity, philanthropy, and justice. To this end it is my desire to direct my feeble efforts. If I may be permitted to set the wedge that more powerful arms than mine shall drive home to the riving of the log of slavery, this is all I ask; for, in so good a cause, to be even allowed to hold the wedge in the right place — in the right end of the log — while others perform the more important part of the duty, is an honour I should be proud of. To point out the proper application of means to the end in this great work, would be glory enough for one life, and I might proceed, without any further remarks, to the elucidation of the subject; but, before doing so, it will be right to examine into some of the reasons why we ought to employ every means in our power, whether public or private, or both combined, in the accomplishment of emancipation. The reasons which would probably press upon us with the most force, might be deduced from studying the calamities brought upon some of the other nations of the earth, both ancient and modern, which have stood in close relation with slavery. By looking at this subject through the experience of these nations, we might perceive, not only our own position and probable fate, but also the right direction of the line of duty, in securing safety and happiness for ourselves. In seeking for this line by the light of historic experience, it is not my intention at present to allude to more than a single example, in proof of the fact that slavery is an evil which ought to be avoided or abolished, in order to avert the calamities which have been, and ever must continue, inseparably connected with it.

In whatever light, for example, we may view the bondage of the house of Jacob, either in a political, moral, or religious sense, one thing is certain, that the mighty hand of God was in it from the beginning, doubtless for the working out the good of mankind upon earth, to the latest generations, provided the great lessons taught in these events should be regarded in their true light by the species. However mysterious it may seem, that the buying of a single man into slavery should bring about, in the course of time, and by a long series of natural and political sequences, a vengeance, through the immediate agency and expressed will of the almighty God, more terrific and appalling than any other event in the history of the world, yet this is a historical fact; and, however incomprehensible it may seem to be from the beginning, the connection of the Israelite with the Egyptian, is, nevertheless, recorded in the book which also lays down the law of man's duty to God; a book which, from that day to this, has been held sacred in the hands of a God-loving and God-abiding people, as prescribing the right rule of conduct towards both the Creator and his creatures.

But the events which led to the final catastrophe

of Egypt, were such that they at once appeal to the comprehensive power of human reason, which has been rendered by the Creator fully competent to fathom the immutable laws of cause and effect — laws bearing alike, and without change, upon all questions throughout the whole moral and physical world. Man, being endowed with an intellect which excites him to the divination of cause and effect, he may analyse seeming mysteries, and aim at the comprehension of the workings of the universe; and he has power to understand all things affecting himself or his interests, for good or for evil. If he err, the only apology which he can make for his errors will be found in the culpable prostitution of his high endowments. Such an apology is but an acknowledgment of wrong.

Once comprehending and acknowledging the great truth, that a combination of like circumstances will produce absolutely and invariably the like effects, then will human reason read the full meaning of Israelitic bondage and Egyptian calamity, as a monument reared by God himself, upon which is inscribed the rule of conduct for nations and individuals; pointing for good in one direction, and towards evil consequences in the other. The oppressor never escapes the punishment of his oppression, nor can benevolence fail to receive the reward of its well-doing; though God employs both for his own wise purposes.

Human reason, then, in all cases in which results are to be divined, erects for itself some standard or law by which it can establish, after making due allowance for variation of circumstances, the proper conclusion or prophetic anticipation, in relation to the truth or fact at which it aims. Hence, in prejudging the necessary results of American slavery, we should at once compare it with the causes and circumstances by which the institution has been surrounded, in other times and other places, in order to arrive at the effects it must inevitably produce hereafter upon both master and slave. Thus, taking Egyptian bondage as a test of slavery, or as a guide to the results of slavery in other places, and, in order to arrive at just and truthful conclusions, we note the prominent facts in relation to it, such as these—Joseph was sold into bondage by his brethren; Joseph, as a slave, performs good service for his masters, and renders to the Egyptians services by which their wealth and comforts are vastly increased above those of the surrounding nations. In the course of time, Joseph's kindred come into Egypt also; they partake of the vast advantages of which the Egyptians are in possession, and remain in the country about four hundred years, all the while improving their condition for the great work to which, as a people, they were appointed. The Egyptians, upon the other hand, were made to prosper and grow rich, by the benefits they derived from the labour of the bondmen, who, from the beginning, advanced rapidly in civilization. With the rapid increase of the numbers of the bondmen, increased the exactions of their masters, in support of idleness, vicious habits, and licentious indulgences, until a separation of master and bondmen took place, bringing with it unspeakable calamities. Here then we have an array of circumstances, all tending to a final separation of master and slave. And if we could find a combination of precisely like circumstances in another place, we should be at no loss in judging of the result.

Should Egypt, however, be raised as a standard by which you would ascertain the probable results of slavery in this or any other country, you would necessarily compare circumstances, and allow for all the modifications, as they should appear more or less aggravating in character.

Thus, when we inquire into the subject of slavery in our own land, we find that the slave brought into this country was bought from his brother; that he rendered himself useful here, to enrich his master; that he laboured here to secure his comforts; that his labours were valuable to such an extent, that his brother was hunted down like a wild beast, upon the soil of his birth, made captive, and brought here to enrich the master. This is an aggravated circumstance compared with anything that occurred in Egypt. He has remained here more than two hundred years; he has increased, by his labour, the wealth of the nation; with the increase of his numbers, and the amount of his labour, increases the desire of the nation to make a display of wealth, and riot in the indulgence of idleness, vice, and licentiousness; and with this desire, like the Egyptians, we exact the full toll of " brick without straw;" nor do we relax in the oppression under which his voice is daily raised on high, calling aloud for a release from bondage. Comparisons are said to be odious, but if we can proceed one step further, and believe that this nation is called upon to release the African from bondage, with as loud a voice as Moses called upon Pharaoh to let his people depart to their own land — if we can believe that they have been allowed to sojourn here for their improvement and their own good, so as to enable them to redeem their own nation from depravity; and if we shall still refuse to make any return for the services they have rendered us — then it alone remains for human reason to draw the conclusion. The result will not appear to be miraculous.

Human reason ought to teach wisdom. So it does. Errors grow out of a wilful disregard of our own experience, and the experience of others. That course of conduct which lowers self-respect, and injures others, is never maintained and persisted in, except from some slavish habit of indulgence that cannot be laid aside without a sacrifice. And if persisted in, such habits grow more pernicious daily. The end is utter depravity and a premature death. Youth aims at good; age too often becomes depraved, and cherishes depravity with all its pernicious influences, for the gratification of self. The child never intentionally practices that which is hurtful to itself, but avoids it. Thus, from the moment its intellect begins to be developed, it judges and reasons from the circumstances which surround it, for good or harm to itself; it learns to love its mother, and all who minister to its comforts, for the good it experiences from them. In all things which give it pain, it immediately reasons upon effect; and whilst it cherishes good, it avoids evil, upon the innate principle of self-preservation. That which is of the most service to it is, that it profits by experience, which mature age often refuses to do. Thus the teachings of babes are worthy to be imitated by men — by nations.

What was it that induced our patriotic sires to establish a representative form of government, except to avoid the evils which follow in the train of despotism? Some of those evils they experienced in themselves, and no higher wisdom than that of the child led them to avoid these in the future. Besides, they had the teachings of history; and in their wisdom they profited by these teachings. Nor was this all: they made sacrifices of all their comforts to attain the highest good for their country, to which they pledged life, fortune, and honour! History cannot point to another and so glorious an example of self-denial. The nations of the future may profit by it, if they are wise. But, to such as are incapable of denying themselves pernicious gratifications, the example will be of no avail, because such sacrifices lie at the root of the example. To the attainment of a highly useful, moral, and honourable standing, the line of conduct for an individual is plainly laid down in the story of our founders. Nor is this line of conduct less strongly marked for a nation.

The great men of the revolution, of whom we are so proud, raised a new standard for the government of a people. Not without an effort — not without hope. The hopes were for good, because they determined in themselves to sacrifice the power which oppressed them from abroad. By their efforts, they had to contend against a determined foreign foe, and the folly, ignorance, and selfishness of too many at home. But, whatever the sacrifices or efforts they may have made, their success elevated them to a point in the temple of fame, where they receive the award of having achieved the highest deeds for humanity. Their history commences a new era in the history of nations. Shall we forget that we are the sons of those self-sacrificing patriots? Shall we be satisfied with the light their glory throws around us, when we too are privileged to make sacrifices, and when humanity pleads as strongly in favour of the oppressed with us as it did with our patriotic progenitors? Shall we forget; I say, shall we forget that we are the sons of such sires? "Honour thy father and thy mother, that thy days may be long in the land which the Lord thy God giveth thee."

If we have received good things from our ancestors, and they are glorified in having obtained them for us, how much will their glory and our own be enhanced by showing to the world that we know how to use them! Let us make the sacrifice which we are called upon to make, in the emancipation of the African race within the United States, and we shall be raised in the temple of fame to a level with our ancestors. It will be seen that the son was not unmindful of the teachings and example set by the father.

What are the sacrifices we shall have to make? Not that of money! I think I can show that emancipating the slave and colonizing Africa will make us richer; as all good works will enhance the riches of an individual. The sacrifices we shall be called upon to make will be in *things which lead to a misapplication of wealth,* in a manner tending to licentious and vicious habits. To guard against such tendencies will always be profitable for a nation.

Is the bondage of Africa in this our favoured land less burdensome than was that in Egypt? No! More bearable in any respect? No! On the contrary, it is of a more aggravated character — severing the closest ties of nature — producing a degree of lamentation that doubtless raises its voice as high as the heavens. Has not the Colonization Society, like Moses in Egypt, supplicated for a return of the children of Africa to their own land? And have we not hardened our hearts against this appeal? And are we not, like Pharaoh, rioting in wealth, and luxury, and licentiousness, by means of the labour of the African, whose "life is made bitter with hard bondage?" The Egyptians had secured wealth sufficient from the labour of the bondman, to have sent him to a land which was, to him, a land of promise. So have *we* wealth by millions, secured to us by the labour of the bondman, all sufficient to send him home. But here let the parallel stop: to carry it further would be to encounter the wrath of the Almighty, to avert which, let us, with one heart and one mind, do what our reason teaches us it would be right to do, and dispose of a little of that wealth which is now squandered in the promotion of idleness, and too often used in securing vicious indulgences, by an appropriation of a part of it for the purpose of sending the Negro home to the land of his fathers.

The history of every nation upon earth which has indulged slavery in its worst forms, is written nearly in the same language, and in one or two sentences: — their rise in wealth and luxury — their progress in licentiousness — and their utter desolation; their whole course only marked by a variety of circumstances, all alike tending to a dishonourable grave. Permit us to hope that the United States will not only avoid this rock of slavery, upon which she may be wrecked, but all other causes which have strong tendencies to subvert empires.

Who can doubt her destiny, if her high mission is controlled by principle?

That nations, like individuals, are in strict accountability to the laws of God, will not be denied. Nor is it necessary or germain to my purpose to cite the many occurrences which have transpired in the downfall and utter desolation of nations, since the days of Egypt, to sustain the position. I claim that a maintenance of sobriety, honesty, justice, humanity, and economy are as necessary to the character of a nation, as the same virtues are to the honourable standing of an individual.

The rise and fall of nations, from the days of Egypt down to the present time, are full of instruction to us. These changes, regulated by the immutable laws of cause and effect, indicate for us the right and straight way wherein we must move, if we would secure to ourselves the power to maintain in pristine vigour the full benefit of our institutions, and to our posterity, upon each succeeding anniversary of our independence, the power to proclaim to all nations of the earth, that man is capable of self-government.

Our theory leaves the individual conscience free to choose the right and eschew the wrong, according to the spirit of Christianity. In a system founded upon such a principle, universal good must prevail;

for, where the citizen is sovereign in all things, and where equal rights are really secured to all, the highest order of human government is attained. But, let the poison of legislative inconsistency deform this system—let equality of rights be trampled under foot in relation to either race or caste—and history teaches another lesson. The worm is then in the bud, and the fruit must wither. The handwriting is on the wall, in characters so bold, that none but the blind, the infatuated, the reckless, can fail to perceive the finger of prophecy, tracing on the sands of time the horrible phantom of desolation, brooding over the grave of power and the ruins of glory. To profit by the experience of nations, is the part of humanity, justice, and common sense. To shun the evils inevitably resulting from profligacy, idleness, and licentious debauchery —the back-blow of the oppressed against the oppressor— is no more the duty of the wise and patriotic, the shrewd and cautious, than a natural prompting of the instinct of self-preservation.

In relation to slavery, there is no period of time in the world's history from which more light can be elicited than the period of the Israelitic captivity; and many of the chief features and consequences of this peculiar example of bondage will apply with startling force to this evil as it now exists in the

United States. That God will assuredly raise a mighty hand for the delivery of the oppressed, now as then; that he will as assuredly punish now as then, the human power that resists his will, when, with the scales of justice in his hand, he thunders from the mercy-seat, "Give freedom to the slave;" that the exodus will follow the genesis, in this great work, and that both are parcels of his one great plan, he that denies is mad. Shall we obey his fiat peaceably while we may? or shall we pursue the pillar of cloud and pillar of flame, to the great *red sea* of our destiny?

That distinct races of men cannot inhabit the same country upon equal terms, and that the violent separation of master and slave carries with it evils of the most terrifying character, are facts which American experience distinctly proves. May we, with anxious solicitude, implore a wise and most merciful God, who has vouchsafed to us so many blessings, and given us such abundant cause for thankfulness, that he may guide us in the right way — a way in which we cannot err — so that we may provide the means for the release of the bondman from captivity. And if we should fail, as a nation, to do all that is in our power for this great end, may He still, in the continuance of this mercy, avert from us evils of such magnitude as despoiled and inundated Egypt; such evils as have connected themselves with the downfall of every other nation upon earth that has fostered slavery beyond the point of the Divine intention; evils which, when measured by the short span of human wisdom, appear to be the result of the violent separation of master and slave. Therefore, whenever this separation shall be determined upon here, reason will dictate for our own benefit, and especially for that of the slave, that it ought to be effected with the mutual consent and approval of all parties interested. Such are the admonitions of history; but even independently of these teachings, self-respect, and the high behests of humanity should be a sufficient inducement for emancipation. We claim to raise a standard of equality in our Government, by which other nations may profit. Let us, then, make our whole conduct worthy of example. It is true, that, as a people, we claim to be highly favoured. We enjoy that liberty by which all are allowed to converse with God, each in his own good time and in his own way, with a conscience free from molestation, *except the poor African*. He alone has no abiding place amongst us, where he can lay down his head, and rest in the consciousness that he too is free to come and go, and enjoy all the blessings by which his fellow men are surrounded. Alas! this is the land where the African (whether bond or free) is bound to render a full account of his brick. His home is not here. He, like the Israelite, must look to a land of promise. But in Africa he, too, will have a nationality of character. May his departure from shores alien and unkind to him alone, render him great and happy in the future!

D

CHAPTER III.

THE PUBLIC DOMAIN A MEANS FOR EMANCIPATION.

Degrading Effects of the Mismanagement of the Public Domain — Description, History, and Extent of the Domain — Abuses and Proper Uses of the Domain — Congress incapable of properly managing the Domain.

If it be our duty to send the African bondman to illuminate the darkness of his fatherland with the moral light which he has acquired from merely looking upon a liberty that he is not permitted to share — if it be our duty to do this with a portion of that wealth to which his compulsory labour has so largely contributed—it behoves us to inquire from what part of the national resources the necessary means can be, or should be appropriated. Let us, with this view, devote the present chapter to the consideration of the extent and character of that richest of all American possessions, the *Public Domain*, and the abuses practised upon it.

When the policy or the construction of a Government gives impunity to outrage, whether from a desire to encourage, or an inability to check it, the tendency of that Government is towards decay and ruin. Already we are prating of the rapid acquisition of territories inhabited by a people differing from us in language and religion — a people who cannot be made readily to understand the spirit of our institutions. What the Government does not attempt, in this direction, the people do; and however lawless may be the manner of satisfying this desire for acquisition by means dishonourable and illegal, the Government cannot, or will not arrest the motion, until the adventurer becomes familiar with lawlessness. The dream of "manifest destiny" (I do not deny that dreams often come true) is causing us to forget that our dominion may be extended beyond the point at which laws can be carried into effect, in a country of immense expansion and sparse population. We are on the point of losing, if we have not already lost, for the time, the power which adds most to the respectability of a nation,— *the power to execute the laws;* also, the far more important power of protecting, as a sacred trust, the interests of the future. To this unhappy consummation we are rapidly approximating; so that, to provide for the licentious will soon be the chief occupation of Government, and individual rights in person or property will soon cease to be maintained.

The lawlessness of the adventurer even now can scarcely be punished, especially for the crime of trespassing upon the territory and robbing the individuals of the adjoining States. Nor is this all. He cannot be reached for putting a whole nation in motion to resist his barbarities, practised against a friendly power. The barbarities which the savages of the American forests have committed upon us, in point of turpitude and crime, fall far short of our unprovoked plunder of a friendly nation, which, though boastful, is too feeble to punish.

When a state will not, or cannot punish depredations upon public property, then, just in proportion to the value of this property, it will be seized upon by the lawless adventurer. He will claim it as his own, independently of all rights of society, and, by an immoral contagion, his example will rapidly contaminate the whole community. The demagogue, who is too often appointed to judge of these rights, and is sworn to administer the fundamental laws of the country justly, pronounces the usurpation warrantable, in order to maintain an ephemeral popularity; and, to this end, regardless of the public good, he will strain his limited ability to legislate for personal advantages, in opposition to the rights of society. Such is our experience in the acquisition of territory. Public lands are, upon this principle of legislation, voted away by our Government for all manner of purposes, upon any and every pretext, regardless of the benefits which the proceeds of these lands would yield, if expended upon objects conducive to the future interests of the people. The right of such a Government to hold out its system as an example to other realms, is gone. As well might the prodigal claim to be an economist: as well might the extortioner claim to be just. The father of a family may permit one son to destroy the property of his neighbour; another, to rob him of his own; a third, to establish himself upon the patrimonial acres, in defiance of his laws for the benefit of the whole family; and altogether, to use up the whole estate in the purchase of as much as it will buy in matters of luxury, and then run in debt. He may do all this, while indulging a morbid desire to give away his lands to every stranger that approaches him! But what should we say to the insane folly of such a parent? Would we allow his proud claim to be a sound practical example to others? It would be folly to hope, on behalf of a nation powerless to enforce its laws for the regulation of property, an escape from the fate which must inevitably fall upon a family governed in defiance of all morality, honesty, justice, and economy.

Wealth, in a nation or an individual, cannot be detrimental where its true value is understood, where it is properly appreciated for its usefulness in supplying present wants and securing future benefits. Thus used, it adds true honour, power, and glory to the nation; it is worse than useless when its application fails to do good, and it is expended in generating evils prejudicial to the best interests of the people.

The question may be asked, honestly and fairly, whether we have not arrived at that point in the progress of our Government, when the wealth of a nation begins to foster evils, such as neither morality nor patriotism can sanction.

Henceforth, the tendency of American glory is downward, unless we come to a pause, and reflect upon the causes which have sunk us already so low; unless we cease to be dazzled by the glare of the expiring lamp — the unnatural accession of glory and power which has invariably marked the approach of the decline of empires, like the glow on the cheek of consumption, which gives a brightness to fading life, but owes its very existence to corruption and decay within.

The time has arrived when the genuine patriot, wherever he may be found—in the halls of Congress, in the capitols of states, the wild forest, the cultivated farm, or the private study, in whose tempered light the abstract thinker calls up the spirits of the buried great, or the poet-seer reads the shadows of coming events — must rally to the rescue. They must unite as one man in seeking out nobler purposes to engage the efforts of our statesmen. ALL! ALL! are bound at this moment,—

"Big with the fate of Cæsar and of Rome,"

which is destined to determine the life or death, the glory or shame, of our country — to aid in the establishment of such a policy as shall give profitable and salutary direction to the wealth, power, and influence of the nation, and check the progress of those social poisons that sparkle to destroy.

Brightest among all our possessions, most tempting, most corrupting, by the struggles it engenders for its divisions and spoils, lies the Public Domain. How shall we convert it from an instrument of corruption and decay, into a lever for effecting sound national advancement.

Of all our national burdens, the curse of slavery stands pre-eminent. To what nobler purpose can we devote a fair share of the proceeds of our almost unlimited possessions, than to the gradual and safe, the *just* removal of that curse? What, then, is the Public Domain?

All the territory of the United States which lies beyond, or outside of the original boundaries of the old thirteen states, except the "Western Reserve," the Virginian Military Reserve in Ohio, and such portions of our more recent acquisitions by purchase or conquest as were legally in the possession of private individuals of a civilized race at the time of annexation, have been part and parcel of the public domain. What is termed the "triangle" in Pennsylvania, (part of the county of Erie,) was also at one time a part of it.* Conflicting titles, growing out of the ignorance of geography at the time of the granting of the royal charters of Massachusetts, Connecticut, New York, Virginia, North Carolina, and Georgia, (nearly all of which claimed from the Atlantic to the Pacific,) covered nearly all the territory west of these states, as far as the Mississippi river, beyond which the claims of France and Spain interfered with all the English titles.†

---

* The "triangle" was claimed by Massachusetts and New York. It was purchased from those states by the United States, and sold to Pennsylvania in 1788, at eighty-seven cents per acre, to give this last-named state a frontier on the lakes.

† New York had an indefinite claim to all the territory west of her limits. Massachusetts and Connecticut claimed all that lay west of their respective borders, to the Pacific, though both were barred by the prior claim of Holland to the New Netherlands, now New York, and hence they were compelled to overleap that state. The

The disputes between the states, growing out of this condition of things, together with the fears of the small states, (especially Maryland, who dreaded the seemingly limitless claim of Virginia, and her impending power,) induced all the claimants to cede their titles to the United States, in trust for the equal benefit of all the states, " and for *no other purpose whatever.*"* Connecticut refused to cede the Western Reserve in Ohio, and was permitted to retain it.

From the states of Massachusetts, New Hampshire, and Virginia, were formed those of Maine, Vermont, and Kentucky. From the lands trans-

---

Connecticut claim also brought this state into conflict with Pennsylvania, and hence the feuds and border wars of Wyoming.

The Virginian claim extended originally westward, at right angles to the coast, and so to the Pacific. Thus it covered the greater part of the lands west of Pennsylvania, north of the Ohio, and east of the Mississippi, to the northern boundary of the United States. Hence all these claims overlapped each other to a vast extent.

* The terms of this part of the deed of cession were as follows:—

"All the lands within the territory so ceded to the United States, and not reserved or appropriated to any of the before-mentioned purposes, or disposed of in bounties to the officers and soldiers of the American army, shall be considered as a common fund for the use and benefit of such of the states as have become, or shall become, members of the confederation or federal alliance of said states, Virginia inclusive, according to their respective proportions in the general expenditures, and shall be faithfully and *bona fide* disposed of for that purpose, and no other purpose whatever."

ferred to the United States, have sprung Ohio, Indiana, Illinois, Michigan, and Wisconsin. By treaties with France and Spain, the annexation of Texas, and conquest from Mexico, we have since acquired vast territories beyond the limits of the first deed of trust, but not the less virtually bound by the same restriction to the equal benefit of all the states. From these have been derived the states of Tennessee, Alabama, Florida, and Mississippi, with all those west of the great river of the same name. The public domain may now be defined to include all the land that is unsold or unappropriated, from the northern boundaries of Mexico and the Gulf, to the 49th degree of north latitude, and from the limits of the thirteen original states, to the Pacific ocean.

I am not enabled to lay my hand upon statistics showing exactly the whole amount of acres within this area; but I shall not be far wrong when I say that it contains seventeen hundred millions of acres, probably three hundred millions of which have been disposed of by adjustment in the settlement of claims, sales, and donations to states for school purposes and improvements, leaving on hand at least fourteen hundred millions of acres, either to be converted into means for effecting national good, or lavished, as is now contemplated by Congress, on actual settlers, as a free gift.*

* Virginia, Massachusetts, and Connecticut ceded 169,609,819 acres; Georgia, 58,898,522 acres; and North and South Carolina, 26,482,000 acres. The domain was enlarged by treaties with Great Britain in 1783 and 1794, and with Spain in 1795 and 1819; with France, in 1803, and with Mexico, in 1848. Before the purchase of Florida, when bounded by 49° N. lat., it was estimated at 1,242,792,673 acres, of which there remained unsold in 1843, 1,084,064,993 acres.

The principal appropriations of land by Congress, prior to 1843, were: — Every sixteenth section in each county, being one thirty-sixth of the whole, to schools in the new states: one-twentieth of the land for roads and other purposes: 6,000,000 acres bounty land in aid of the war with England, with special grants to refugees from Canada and Nova Scotia; to the State of Ohio, for internal improvements; and miscellaneous grants to General Lafayette, &c., in all amounting to about 33,000,000 acres. New York ceded in 1781; Virginia, in 1784; Massachusetts, in 1785; Connecticut, in 1786; South Carolina, in 1787; and Georgia, in 1802. Congress commenced legislating on the public lands in 1776; but the states claimed the right of soil as well as jurisdiction, and objected to the Congressional action till the cessions were completed.

Connecticut reserved to herself a tract, (the Western Reserve,) bounded by 41° N. lat., and extending west, from the Pennsylvania line, 120 miles. Virginia stipulated for a security for the old French settlers on her claim, and reserved two tracts, one of 150,000 acres near the rapids of the Ohio, the other, known as the Military Reserve, between the little Miami and Sciota rivers, for her soldiers of the Revolution. Georgia and South Carolina ceded the Mississippi Territory, from N. lat. 31° to N. lat. 35°, east of the Mississippi, Georgia receiving therefor 1,250,000 dollars. Georgia also stipulated for the extinction of the Indian titles by the United States.

This property has been acquired by conquest and purchase, at a vast sacrifice of blood and treasure. How this trust is carried out, we shall see. Thus far, all the money received for land which has been sold, falls far short of the price it cost, in wars, in extinguishing Indian titles, in surveying, and in fees to land officers and Indian agents. The balance has been paid by a tax, bearing upon each citizen alike; yet, Congress has it now in contemplation to give the land away to one class of citizens only!

This domain was looked upon, in the early history of the Government, as constituting a fund of inexhaustible riches, for carrying into effect objects of vast interest to the people, and, at the same time, freeing them from burdensome taxes. There is a value in this domain, if properly applied, which would relieve taxation in many important ways. With views such as these in regard to the public domain, laws were passed, immediately upon the adoption of the Constitution of the United States, for regulating the mode of securing the title to the purchaser; and the price was fixed at a rate deemed just, both towards purchaser and seller. But it was soon found that in the passage of those laws, neither the true interests of the domain nor those of the public were yet understood.

The first sales of land by the Government were,

1,000,000 of acres to John Symes & Co., exclusive of two sections for religious purposes; a like number to the Ohio Company, and 267,000 acres to the State of Pennsylvania—all at sixty-seven cents per acre. Part of the first two grants, however, reverted, from the inability of the purchasers to meet their engagements in full. No other sales were made in less quantities than by townships or entire sections, upon a credit, in four annual instalments, at two dollars per acre. That which gave peculiar value to contracts under these early enactments was, that the Government obliged itself to extinguish all Indian and other titles, to survey the lands, and to set durable landmarks, so that when the purchaser laid down his money, he received an indisputable and perfectly clear title. There was no clashing of boundary lines.

Changes, with regard to terms of sale and payment, have since been made, but the system of location and title remains the same to this hour. How pleasant such an arrangement must seem to the man who has paid the earnings of his whole life to lawyers, in order to secure his land, under the land warrant act of Virginia, in the Military Reserve in the State of Ohio, where no such security of title exists! The effect of this system, which allowed each man to claim and survey his own warrant, was to cause boundary lines to overlap, like shingles in the roof of a house. It was soon found that, for the benefit of the purchaser, land should be sold in less quantities than by townships, or even sections. Sales of half and quarter sections were then legalized, and land offices were established. But even the quarter sections were speedily ascertained to be inconveniently large; and it was also discovered that the credit system did not work well. It so encumbered with debt the settlers of a new country which had scarcely any roads, and no outlets to market, except the long sweep of the Mississippi river to the city of New Orleans, that they had no ability to pay. The Government, claiming to be just, and exacting justice in turn, caused a vast deal of hardship in the endeavour to collect the instalments due on such purchases. When it was found impracticable, compromises were resorted to; and, in view of this difficulty, other regulations were adopted which cannot be surpassed for their simplicity and practical utility. The law of 1820 repealed all other laws in relation to the sale of land, except those that go to secure the most admirable title to the purchaser, and to regulate the penalties that had been provided from the beginning against trespassing upon public property. These penalties were increased, and the United States Marshal was required, by law, more strictly to enforce them. At this time, (only thirty-four years ago,) these laws were generally respected; and where they were not, the penalty was exacted; and this continued to be the case, without opposition or complaint upon the part of the people, until the administration of General Jackson, when pre-emption laws, passed in the year 1832, led to the defiance of the national authority, to frauds upon the Government, by obtaining land under false pretences, and to trespasses upon the rights of future purchasers; which outrages were perpetrated with impunity. The pre-emption law required the raising of a crop to secure the legality of the claim; yet the spirit of the law was evaded by the speculator. A small portion of land would be enclosed, say within four pannels of fence, by two persons living at a distance: wheat would then be sown therein. Next harvest, the speculators would return, and find a stalk or two of grain growing. They would rub this grain from the chaff, and call it harvesting! Thus, by complying with the letter of the law, in violation of its spirit, they settled their consciences in swearing each other into a claim of one hundred and sixty acres each! No doubt evasions of the law contemplating the free gift of homesteads, will be practised by the speculator in like manner, if that law should be enacted.

What a value the land must possess, that will induce such contemptible frauds! Much of the land claimed in this way would have brought ten dollars per acre at a fair public sale. Does this not prove, to the full conviction of every right-minded man, the high value of this Domain, considered by the Government so worthless now, as to be solely the object of a free gift?

Under the pre-emption law, the fraudulent practices against the future purchasers were effected after this manner: a man would establish a claim to a lot of one hundred and sixty acres, partly wood and partly prairie; he would then cut rails upon the public property to fence in this said lot, regardless of the legal penalties enjoined in such cases. What is the practice of the Government in the enforcement of these penalties now? In the North, she commands the marshal to enforce them whenever he can find the plunderer of pine logs; and if caught, the culprit is obliged to pay the penalty in some way or other; whilst in Utah or California she permits the squatter to plunder and lawlessly riot upon the public property with impunity. Is this even justice? Would it not be better and more honourable, under such circumstances, to abrogate altogether the laws enjoining penalties?

When the idea of giving away 1,000,000,000 acres

of land is boldly held out, and we call to mind the mismanagement of the public land trust for the last twenty years, surely it may be charged against Congress that, in this matter, it has been an unfaithful steward. How much does this recent neglect of a great public interest contrast with the care and caution of the Congress of 1820, in relation to the same trust! Then, a law was passed, requiring that the whole of the land should be surveyed into eighty acre lots; and that each lot should first be offered for sale by public outcry, and sold to the highest bidder. This law enacted penalties against all manner of conspiracies to prevent a fair sale. After the vendue, the land offered, but remaining unsold, was registered in the land office, subject to be sold in any required quantities, by proper officers appointed for this purpose. It was also provided that any citizen should be allowed to purchase any lot of forty acres which he might prefer, after making oath that he would never again make a like application. It is obvious that this privilege might embarrass or prevent the sale of a section to which a selected lot belonged, especially when the remainder of the section happened to be inferior in quality or position; but, for the benefit of the man who had only fifty dollars with which to buy a clear title to forty acres, he was allowed the privilege at all risks

E

of inconvenience or loss to the Government. Fifty dollars for forty acres of land! only think of it! The land my eyes now rest on, as I gaze though the small window before which I write, bears a taxation annually more than equal to this price! Who would not, when plunder is thought disreputable, rather purchase a title at such a rate than be classed with beggars? How much better would it be for the whole people, and the poor man himself, if the Government had steadily enforced this law, without the false pretence of sympathy for the poor, which is now so strongly professed by the demagogue and speculator on land as well as upon the Presidency! It must be seen that the law might have been made to extend to a twenty acre lot, for the benefit of the poor man. Twenty acres for twenty-five dollars! would this have been a hardship? Certainly not; for, the land upon the Public Domain is equal in value to any other land upon earth, and twenty acres, properly cultivated, will support a large family anywhere. Even in the forest it will do it; and, just in proportion to the growth of a dense population in the neighbourhood around, it increases in value. Twenty acres make a large farm in the neighbourhood of cities. Besides, I have known men who have lived upon six hundred and forty acres, without having cleared up and brought under cultivation as much as twenty acres. The whole of this free homestead mania, when honestly exhibited, is the result of a false sympathy, and goes to enrich one class of the community at the expense of others.

Is it not time to look after an interest covering hundreds of millions of dollars, that can be applied in such a manner as to benefit substantially every citizen, and entail rich blessings on the future, all, all alike, participating in its benefits as they stand alike in sovereignty of citizenship? Such is the value and quality of the means I would in part apply to cure the evil of slavery.

The Public Domain includes gold mines that ought, on every principle of justice, to be secured to the nation; for, so long as no equivalent is paid for the use of those mines by one citizen, it is unjust in the extreme to punish another for trespassing upon pine or oak timber lands; as is done in many regions without mercy. So soon as means, growing out of the territories, shall be made applicable to high philanthropic objects, and others of general import, then, a rent should be exacted for these mines.

I think I have shown that in the Public Domain we possess all the power and means necessary to emancipate the slave in a manner equally consistent with the interests of servant and master, the north and the south.

In my plan for the application of these means, I intend to show that the nation will be invigorated by the measure, and that its benefits will be distributed among all the citizens alike, and in just proportion. I shall take occasion also to demonstrate, still more forcibly, that the Homestead Bill, now before Congress, is not based upon charity, humanity, honesty, or justice. The false pretences and sophistry, upon the strength of which this bill is urged, together with the whole disgraceful management by Congress of so vast a trust, leaves not a doubt upon my mind of the *unfitness of Congress for the management of the Public Domain.* To prevent the evils and moral deformity growing to most gigantic dimensions out of this mismanagement, (which need but to be rightly examined to shock the whole nation,) was the motive that prompted this inquiry. The remedy—the result—I have written down and printed.

Almost my whole life has been spent in the open air, in field and forest, sometimes looking upon and commiserating the wrongs heaped upon the poor Indian, and, at the same time, observing the frauds committed upon the Government by the lawless adventurer, setting aside in his profligacy law, justice, and humanity. I have been all the while rather observing and noting those scenes by which I was surrounded, than studying the graces of literature, with a view to their presentment in a captivating dress. Unused to the practice of the pen, I would wish you, reader, to judge me rather by what I say and mean, than by the mere manner and style in which I have said it.

I desire to see the appropriation of the Public Domain made in accordance with the simplest principle of common sense, such as actuates the boy who picks rags out of the gutter, looking into the future for wealth and competence, intelligence and respectability for his family! To this end, he does not clothe himself with these rags. He washes them, and has them rendered into paper upon which the value of millions may be stamped. How this poor boy would scandalize himself by covering his body with these rags! Would a similar policy be worthy of the nation that claims to lead the van in the march of civilization and philanthropy? Yet such is precisely our policy in relation to the public lands. Citizens of a glorious Republic, with whom lies all the power, let us change the disgraceful system. Let us take our noble estate out of the hands of agents unworthy of the trust. But how? In the next chapter, we shall see.

CHAPTER IV.

PLAN FOR CONSTITUTIONALLY REMOVING THE PUBLIC DOMAIN FROM THE CUSTODY OF CONGRESS.

Proposed Convention of the People for considering the Public Domain as a means for Emancipation and other great National Purposes—Plan for the Organization of a Board of the Public Domain—Propriety of encouraging Public Works in Africa—Hints on Negro Education, in anticipation of the Exodus—"The Redemption System" in Africa—Appropriations to American Public School Funds, with collateral extinction of the State Debts, and the encouragement of State Improvements—Folly of the Free Homestead Scheme—How to prevent injury to the South from the Exodus—Amplitude of the Resources from the Domain, if properly guarded—Beneficial results to Agriculture, Commerce, Currency, and Morals—Tendency of California Gold to extend Slave Territory—Further Remarks on the Free Homestead Scheme.

AT the close of the last chapter, I stated the conclusion, legitimately drawn from a long history of abuses, that if the proceeds of the Public Domain are to be wisely appropriated to truly national purposes, and especially to the ultimate removal of the curse of slavery, the public lands *must be taken from the guardianship of Congress*, and placed, by the people, in hands capable of properly administering the trust.

In effecting this object, I would propose that the people, in their majesty, should insist that Congress should pass a law, providing for the election of one citizen from each congressional district in the United States, to meet in convention in Washington upon any appointed day after the 4th of March, 1855, for the purpose, in the first instance, of deciding the simple questions, Whether it be right and expedient that measures for the ultimate emancipation and colonization of the coloured race in this country should be now prospectively provided for; and whether the principal or the interest of the proceeds of the public lands should be, wholly or in part, appropriated to the accomplishment of this purpose, without detriment to the rights of the owner of the slaves.

Should the convention decide these questions in the negative, its labours would cease by the absence of further matter for deliberation : but, let us suppose the people of the United States, thus in formal and lawful convention assembled, to have resolved that it would be right and expedient to commence and complete the emancipation of the slave in the course of the next hundred years, if it should require that length of time to do so wisely and safely; moreover, that, in the Public Domain, we possess the required means. Then, with a view to set aside all manner of doubt that the revenues growing out of at least the interest of the proceeds of this domain will be permanently applied to this and other equally noble purposes, the convention should appoint, or determine the manner of choosing the proper number of persons, of the right character and standing, to regulate and effect the sales of the public lands, just so fast as the United States shall extinguish Indian titles; to manage the proper investment of the same; and to apply the proceeds thereof to the several objects of national importance which may be designated by the convention. These trustees, composing a BOARD OF THE PUBLIC DOMAIN, should have a written constitution, in which their precise duties must be laid down and defined in such a manner that the limits of their power cannot be misunderstood, or its action misapplied. The plan which I propose is, that at least one person, not less than fifty years of age, shall be elected by the people of each state, as a member of the *Board of the Public Domain*, which board shall be invested with ample power to receive the proceeds of sales, and attend to the disbursement of the same. That not more than one-half of the proceeds of any one year should be applied to purposes of emancipation in that year; and moreover, that no larger number of negroes, whether freemen or slaves, should be forwarded to Africa by the board, at any time, than would be likely to find employment and comfortable subsistence there: that, out of this moiety, $100,000 or even a larger sum, should be deposited with the Liberian Government annually, so long as the people of Liberia shall be willing to accept it, upon condition that they consent to tax themselves, and pay in support of their common and agricultural schools, six per cent. per annum upon these donations. This sum, judiciously invested in public improvements, especially railroads leading into the interior of Africa, or in steamboats to run upon their important rivers, would soon begin to produce such striking effects upon the civilization of Africa, and bring such an amount of African products to Liberia, as to offer a powerful inducement to the more wealthy portion of our free coloured population to seek the means of comfort, prosperity, and freedom in Africa. This movement would naturally be followed by a desire on the part of the coloured men generally, to leave a land in which social inequality presents a hopeless barrier against their elevation above virtual serfdom. Thus, by means so small, yet so encouraging, would Liberia, in her improvements, increase her resources and her commerce to such an extent, that she would soon find means within herself for the support of all slaves that it might be found desirable to send her, and all freemen of colour that could not be restrained from going. The labour-saving power of railroads is such that, in the civilization of Africa, they cannot be dispensed with. This, the free and wealthy black of American experience, would soon discover. He would soon find the educated native African, educated by him, quite ready to aid him in such a scheme; and, to carry it forward, he would require little more than tools, and a sufficient number of American coloured engineers and labourers to direct or assist in the construction of public works. To favour this end, measures ought to be immediately adopted to secure to a number of intelligent blacks a practical engineering education that would enable them not only to accomplish such works, but also to conduct like schools in the country of their fathers.

All that is essential in the case of railroads or any other great undertaking in Africa, is simply to start the race in the right course, with ship-builders, bricklayers, carpenters, blacksmiths, masons, &c. They will then soon help themselves, and year after year hold out stronger and stronger inducements to the American African to migrate. Africa has far less need of much money than of proper encouragement and advice. With these, the resources of Africa would soon elevate her civilized people above the necessity of further assistance; and the influence of our kind regard for them, displayed in this effective manner, would tend to ennoble them and raise their self-esteem, while imbuing them with affection towards the land of their former oppression, but present benefaction; and placing that land on the footing of the most favoured nation in their future and invaluable trade. With feelings such as would then inspire them, and with the rapid increase of numbers yearly arriving from America, they would speedily enlarge the boundaries of their civilization and the circle of their affiliated states. Thus they would continue to make progress, until the continent itself would become redeemed from the darkness and depravity that have degraded it to the dust for ages. With such guidance and such encouragement, who can foresee, or even imagine what Africa may become in the short space of three generations?

But, in the furtherance of this good work, we should establish, in every state of the Union in which the black man may be found, institutions where the coloured orphan, or the children of the idle, the convict, the drunkard, and all such as fail to give their children moral instruction, should be gathered together, and taught such things as would be most suited to their capacity; and such among them as display superior talent, girls as well as boys, should be so instructed as to fit them for teachers in the common schools of Africa. Lads of less marked ability should be bound out to farmers and mechanics, where proper places could be found; the girls should be sent into families where they could be taught house-keeping. As these unfortunates become fitted for usefulness, they should be sent to Africa. These schools would afford opportunities to thousands of humane slave-holders, (and I know many such men,) to offer at the altar of humanity children that are often but a source of anxiety and care to them.

A union of sentiment upon the destiny of the *American* African being once established, it may readily be perceived how the feelings of all would harmonize. The young would be offered in not inconsiderable numbers as a free gift, as being the most effective in the work of emancipation. The current of an enlightened emigration of negroes from America to Liberia once established, a daily-increasing commerce would enlarge the resources of Africa. Her merchants, like our own in the days of "the redemption system," would then invite the emigrant as a source of profit; and his passage the resident employer would gladly pay, in return for limited service. Thus immigration would continually increase the agricultural productiveness of the country, and enhance its export trade, its national wealth, and the number of ships and steamboats which would be required for the African trade; so that, from that moment, emancipation and commerce would progress side by side, and all barriers to national advancement would soon disappear.

Thus fairly started by our advice and assistance on the march of a higher destiny, the colonies of civilized negroes would become the most powerful propagandists for the civilization of the savage tribes of the interior, and, as Christianity is the only true foundation for social improvement, Africa would find in her public schools, established upon a portion of the proceeds of the Public Domain, and organized on the American model, the supply of Christian teachers required to redeem the whole continent from its depraved condition, and elevate the people to such rank among the nations as the untrammelled mental and physical power of the race may enable it to reach. No doubt this great work will be cordially promoted by every Christian communion. All Christian sects will vie with each other in educating blacks of superior ability, to carry the gospel to this now heathen land.

To look at the present degradation of Africa, and the past history and present state of American slavery—the one presenting the depth of depravity, the other a story of multitudinous wrongs—it might seem that both these evils had reached a maturity that nothing could relieve — that no human power could now change the destiny of either. But when we consider the immense resources to be realized from a moiety only of our public lands; when we reflect upon the effects of spontaneous advancement in Africa; the result of Christianity, education, agriculture, commerce, and public improvements — all started and facilitated by such ample, nay, superabundant means — why should we hesitate to wipe from our national escutchion every trace of the wrongs we have inflicted on the African race? Why, with these means in our hands, should we resist the voice of the Almighty, and oppose his scheme by saying of this ponderous exodus, *It shall not take place?*

Having now examined how one-half of the proceeds of the Public Domain can be best applied for the benefit of the black man, (and when annually applied under the direction of such a board as has been proposed, who can doubt its sufficiency or beneficial results?) let us inquire what the other moiety, directed by the same wisdom, is capable of doing for ourselves. A portion of these means should be divided annually and pro-rata among the several states, upon the condition that the states should appropriate six per cent. upon the amount deposited, to the support of *their own common schools.* How would this rule work? In Pennsylvania this money would be best used, at first, in buying her debt of forty millions. It is true that the interest would still have to be paid, at least for a time; but with this difference — much of this interest now accrues to foreign bond-holders, which would be paid, under this new system, to the schoolmaster; the principal being invested in the school fund.

As the management of the Public Domain is supposed in this plan to be taken entirely and finally *out of the hands of Congress,* and regulated by commissioners of the states, each state, through its representative in the board, would secure its own equitable interest in the proceeds. Now, whenever the pro-rata share of any state should be found to exceed the most liberal demands of the school fund, the increase of this fund might be arrested, and the future dividends devoted, with the consent and approval of the board, to other purposes of the highest interest to the state or the nation. Among such purposes might even be the extinguishment of the state debts to the school fund, by the appropriation of these future dividends to its credit in other secure investments. Pennsylvania is now paying a heavy state tax, and an almost equally heavy school tax. The effect of such a measure, in progress of time, would be *to remove the necessity of all state tax ;* and similar or equivalent benefits would be conferred upon every state in the Union, both old and new. Thus would be brought about the just execution of the original trust, and the distribution of the proceeds of the public lands, among all the legitimate owners. Will any honest man now contend for the giving away of these lands, upon the plea *that the houseless poor must first* be made *rich,* before the removal of ignorance, the securing of public morals, the defence of the country, or the expenses of wars are at all provided for? Shall we pursue a policy that must continually create pauperism, merely for the purpose of enriching the pauper when created? In order to accomplish this insane, if not wicked purpose, shall we forever deprive ourselves of the only means for accomplishing the peaceful emancipation of the negro, and leave to our children the horrible inheritance of a servile war? Such madness must one day enthrone within the Capitol "the Abomination of Desolation!"

I must now draw the attention of the reader to an all-important consequence of the African exodus, when the numbers of the American slaves become seriously diminished. With the diminution of labourers, labour will be enhanced in value, unless the natural growth of the white, should keep pace with the decrease of the black race. Be this as it may, the great staple of the South must be embarrassed for a time, by the removal of a class of unpaid labourers thought to be peculiarly adapted to its culture. It is not impossible that the cheap *peon* labour of Mexico might in part or entirely supply the deficiency, if, as is probable, necessity or uncurbed ambition should bring that country under the shadow of the stars and stripes, and charge us with the protection of another race, stronger than, and fully as economical as the Chinese, and equally incapable of amalgamating with our own. But, in any case, the cotton of America is destined to inevitable competition with that of civilized Africa, where an enlarged production and a more fitting climate may render that competition formidable. Prudence, then, requires that the friends of eventual emancipation should look around in time for other and not less profitable species of labour, and other staples, to fill up the partial vacuum to be created by our scheme. It strikes me that the substitution of mining and manufacturing operations for a portion of deficient agricultural employment, would furnish the most effective remedy for the evil; and among these, the manufacture of iron holds the first place. The vast quantity of this metal consumed in our own country would afford, in itself, a very heavy operation; but Africa, at every step of her progress, would open new markets for iron; and, with her advancement, the market would become almost unbounded. It may become proper, at some future day, to offer, out of the portion of the proceeds of the public lands appropriated to our own uses, at least a temporary bounty on iron, so adjusted as to enable us to undersell foreign iron in our own market, until home competition shall so reduce the price of manufacture, as to save us, in our own supply, at least as much per ton as the amount of the bounty; a result which experience proves to be ultimately certain. By sending iron to Africa, we should receive in return products which, while enriching us, would largely assist us in remunerating Europe and other countries for the products we should require from them. Trade thus established would render us much more independent than to be continually obliged to demand supplies of a manufactured article, even from nations dependent upon us for the raw material; but when the raw material is refused, and yet the foreign manufacturer forces his merchandise upon us while we possess the raw material in inexhaustible quantity, the policy is disgraceful to our own character for energy and enterprise. *Home competition* is the only power that can permanently diminish prices, and free us from foreign extortion. Nor need I add one word to show that, if means drawn out of the public lands be wisely appropriated in favouring this competition, the benefits resulting from the measure will be equitably felt by every citizen; and, of all staples, iron is the most universal in its application.

But this measure should address itself with peculiar force to the South; for it would cause furnaces to be established in the very places where the vacuum created by emancipation and colonization would be most sensibly felt. Virginia, Maryland, Kentucky, Tennessee, North Carolina — all admirably supplied with the deposits of iron—would erect them in every direction. These would prove highly incentive to other operations. Indeed, every department of business would be enriched by the growth of this manufacture.

There are also other mechanical pursuits which might be made greatly to assist in filling up the vacuum in labour to be produced by the exodus of the negro. To say nothing of those which call into use the great staples of cotton and wool — with the vast importance of which the South, from Virginia to Georgia, is already so familiar — I think that a certain amount of bounty upon the manufacture of silk would be found greatly to the advantage of those regions best adapted to the culture of the worm, (among which, North Carolina stands preeminent,) as well as to those neighbourhoods where the machinery might be located. This measure of temporary assistance to young and struggling manufactures escapes entirely the objections urged by politicians of the school which opposes protective duties as calculated to raise prices upon the consumer; for the obvious effect of bounties is to diminish prices even before home competition has reduced them to a minimum; and, in the plan I advocate, these bounties are drawn from a source which Congress is strongly endeavouring to squander in a manner worse than useless. Under the influence of enterprise directed towards such objects as are suggested, the farm would grow into value beside the furnace; and the factory and the garden, in the neighbourhood of the village: and nothing would remain to make us afraid that an act of moral justice might cause the desolation of our country or our home! Thus, the proceeds of the Public Domain may be applied to the noblest and most useful purposes connected with the honour, prosperity, and pecuniary interests of the whole country, and, at the same time, promotive of its morals and corrective of its corruptions. With what patience, then, can we regard the folly that would devote to the beggar-making gift of free homesteads to the worthless and the idle, a treasure such as this!

Vast as the resources of this domain will undoubtedly be, even independently of any tax upon gold mines, if the national estate be husbanded and conducted on the principles which govern private affairs, (more than sufficient as they would unquestionably prove for any scheme which has yet been devised or dreamed of by American statemen,) we should not conceal from ourselves the fact, that even the most ample resources must be severely taxed in carrying out the emancipation and deportation of 3,500,000 slaves without injustice to the master; for the idea is not to be tolerated that the nation should ask any portion of its citizens to sacrifice upon the altar of liberty, or, if you please, the shrine of abstract justice, that which has descended to them from their ancestors as property, secured to them as such by the Constitution itself — that which, though forced upon them originally by a tyrannical power, in spite of their remonstrances, now constitutes their necessary means of subsistence and comfort. Before the African can be sent by the people to the home of his fathers, his master must be remunerated for the loss of his services; and no small totality of millions will suffice for so enormous a demand. The vastness of the Domain is, therefore, no apology for exempting the gold mines on the public lands of California from all charge, while we protect by law the white pines of the north-west and the live-oaks of Florida. At first, even the interest of the proceeds of the sales of land may be sufficient for our scheme of American and African education, and the little streams of budding colonization; but when Africa is ready, and the torrent of emancipation begins to fill its banks, the drain upon this national estate will be such that it behoves us to be careful of all just income, and California can claim no proper exemption from restraints elsewhere established to check the plunder of the public. No doubt, thus husbanded, the public lands — continually rising in value, like the Sibylline leaves, by the very fact of their diminution — would ultimately produce more than a sufficiency for all the demands of education, colonization, proper bounties on certain manufactures, and the extinguishment of existing state debts. But the present amplitude of the national wealth is no reason for squandering upon one or two generations, in an irrational and demoralizing manner, the rich inheritance of the future.

In carrying out our scheme, before any considerable appropriations in the form of bounties will be found necessary, except for iron, the proceeds of the sales of public lands will have merged in the school funds the amount of the indebtedness of the states whose finances are encumbered, and will have brought other equivalent advantages to those more happily circumstanced. This will be the natural result of the slow progress and slender financial demands that emancipation must of necessity make in the beginning; because the march of improvement in Africa will be slow at first, and these demands must always be made to depend upon the progress of the exodus; and, as has been already suggested, it would be wrong to crowd into Africa more persons, either freemen or emancipated slaves, than can find there proper employment and the means of comfortable subsistence. But it would be folly in us to permit a vigilant rival to secure the initiative in the future market for the great staple of iron, by means of her present power to undersell us, in consequence of the low price of labour with her. In order to prevent this unfortunate result, it will be proper to encourage iron manufactures in America by a suitable bounty from the commencement of operations. At first, then, and for many years, the moiety of the proceeds of the Public Domain will be sufficient to meet all the necessities of emancipation, direct or collateral, immediate or prospective. But, as African civilization advances, temporary bounties on other branches of manufacture will become important to the encouragement of our trade with her. These will increase the demands upon the proceeds of the domain; but the fund thence derivable will be so vast, under an honest and equitable administration of nearly 1,400,000,000 acres, that its division into two equal proportions, as suggested, would, if continued, soon prove burdensome to the states; for all pecuniary surplusages are temptations to corruptions which neither statesmen nor private individuals are always able to resist. This would be the case as soon as the amount of debts of indebted states should be merged in the school-fund, and the school-tax obliterated by the investment of further dividends if required. The desire for additional appropriations to the states would then be gradually diminished, and a larger sum could be conveniently deposited to meet the expenses of the increasing exodus. Moreover, whatever demands might hereafter be made upon this fund by the states, from time to time, we find, in the proposed arrangement for the administration of this trust, the safest means of properly determining such questions, and securing the general and equitable interests of all. It is not to be supposed that a body of grave representatives from the several states, (all men over fifty years of age, of the highest intellect, and the most enlarged experience,) would permit the resources entrusted to their care to be perverted to corrupt purposes, or subjected to individual embezzlement.

The plan which I propose is also of the highest importance in another point of view. The disposition of this vast fund derived from the Public Domain, regulated in the manner suggested, will give the yield of gold, now one of the staples of the country, a direction different from that which it takes at present. It will find permanent and profitable investment in the promotion of agriculture and manufactures — the material of wealth and trade—instead of giving mere temporary facilities to trade, tempting the trader to wild speculations, engendering in the public alternate paroxysms of extravagance and ruinous collapse, from the general ignorance of the true principles of finance.

The application of this gold to commerce, the chief direction now given to it, has a tendency to render the cotton-growing states especially subservient to the foreign manufacturer, and binds the slave-holder by his immediate interests with such pertinacity to the infatuation of commerce, that he forgets that there is any labour in the country worth the protection of our Government, except slave labour; also neglecting the fact that a war of two or three years with Great Britain would render this labour profitless to himself, and the labourer a burden to the community, until the growth of domestic manufactures should create an increased demand for labour throughout the country, so as once more to raise cotton above the condition of a drug.

The causes of decay are spread throughout the universe, and their ultimate power cannot be resisted:—nature will ultimately enforce her laws:—but, in cases in which pernicious influences act upon the prosperity of a nation or an individual, it becomes the duty of man to resist their deleterious agency, by legitimate or rational means. Keeping in mind this solemn truth, let us examine how this California gold is now affecting the interests of the nation.

This gold, at present, cannot be said to yield wealth, for the reason, that it is chiefly expended in the purchase of such articles as are of immediate consumption, or are destructible in a short time. It encourages, in this manner, a display of wealth and luxury, without creating any lasting benefits. It encourages us to purchase all that promotes habits of show and indulgence; consequently, it tends to the increase of idleness, and to broad distinctions between the rich and the poor, political corruption, and social demoralization. The injury done to the nation by these means, is like that which is often witnessed in a family that prides itself upon the wealth which enables it to purchase all that it wants, almost without exertion. How often do we see the children of such a family rendered idle, profligate, and vicious in their habits, and finally dissipating their entire patrimony! We almost always observe that the sons of men whose lives have been passed in the dignified independence which labour yields, are precisely those who stand firmest in support of the honour, dignity, and independence of the nation.

The California gold also reacts most essentially upon slavery — our most perplexing national question — and upon the value of our Public Domain. It clinches the despotism of the former, and promotes the profligate squandering of the latter. It clinches slavery by inflating commerce, and it aguments the means for the immediate purchase of mere luxuries from abroad. The increased amount of foreign fabrics imported upon the strength of the credit derived from this staple, especially of fabrics composed of cotton, which exceed almost all other importations in value, increases the demand for the results of foreign labour, to the disadvantage of national industry. This, in turn, increases the foreign orders for crude cotton. The unnaturally stimulated growth of this branch of trade has the effect of enlarging the income from slave labour, and consequently prompts the slave owner to make strong efforts for the extension of slave territory. To these efforts he is at all times induced by two powerful, selfish motives: the one, the accumulation of personal wealth; the other, the maintenance of an influence in the Government equal to that of the free states, by the aid of a constitutional provision for a slave representation. By such means, he hopes so to control the operation of the commercial wealth of the country, as to render permanent the high value of slave labour, although he cannot escape the conviction that the continuance of the policy he pursues must inevitably prostrate the industry and moral condition of the whole community.

Finding that the California gold, together with duties on excessive importations of foreign products additionally stimulated thereby, now more than supplies all the demands upon the national treasury, the short-sighted people urge upon Congress the free gift of the Public Domain to adventurers, in order that the present state of trade may be the more readily continued. Such are the effects of the policy pursued by the Government, that, if persisted in, we shall find, on the one hand, the Public Domain given over to foreign mendicants, and, on the other, slave labour fostered to the exclusion of the free industrial pursuits of the nation.

When the riches of the Public Domain are properly examined, it becomes difficult to account for the propensity manifested by the Congress of the United States to entertain every project that tends to promote an unjust, unequal, and unrighteous disposition of it, unless upon the supposition that Congress is a body whose constitutional organization *unfits it for the proper management* of so valuable and so peculiar an estate. Of all the wild projects it has yet entertained, this Homestead Bill is the most unjust in all its bearings. Its injustice to the mechanic, and to all classes of citizens not engaged in agriculture, is too obvious for comment; but it cannot claim equity, even towards the agriculturalist. A farmer with his sons, residing at a distance from the Domain, cannot be expected to leave his farm and go to this Domain for the sake of the additional land, upon which he must reside five years to acquire an honest title; nor will he be disposed to send his sons there, at the sacrifice of home associations; but one living upon the Domain already, can claim, without inconvenience, one hundred and sixty acres for himself, and as much more for each of his sons. The project does not present one single honest feature. It is dishonest from its very inception. Independently of the immoral bearing of this measure, in effecting an unjust distribution of the land itself, it is marked by another feature of injustice, which I desire the people of Pennsylvania and all the old thirteen states to look at and examine closely. I have stated that the existing laws in relation to the public lands have required, from the first, that the Indian title should be extinguished, and an indisputable title rendered to the purchaser. This measure I claimed to be of the highest importance. Now, upon giving the land away, one of two things must happen: either these vital facilities must be continued at the expense of the Government, or the recipient of the land must seek his title in the best way he can, and be obliged to rest it upon a personal claim, marking his own boundaries, which I understand to be the practice upon the gold lands. The former course is the only one that can secure the claimant from interminable litigation, growing out of conflicting claims. It is also the only way in which the recipient can be effectually bound to the five years' occupation which the bill before Congress requires, before granting a patent; for how could such occupation be proved, if the location of the claim were left indeterminate? At first sight, it seems reasonable enough that the Government should take action for the security of the recipient of "a free homestead," though it reaps no direct advantage from the settler; but it must be remembered that the actual expense of surveying and locating grants alone, will not fall far short of forty cents an acre, and *you must be taxed* for the coat you wear, and the iron in the plough you follow, in order to pay the necessary expenses incurred for the pleasure of giving away land to the adventurous speculator and the beggar!

When you discover that this charge, in the process of time, must run through the survey of nearly 1,400,000,000 of acres, I sincerely hope that you will begin to think, with me, that the people had better *take this vast trust out of the hands of Congress*, and appoint, as I have suggested, a board, composed of representatives from each state, having power to apply the proceeds of sale to the emancipation of the slave, the extinction of state and school tax, and other great measures for the common benefit of the whole people.

CHAPTER V.

FIRST DUTIES OF THE BOARD OF THE PUBLIC DOMAIN IN RELATION TO THE EXODUS.

Preparation of Africa for the reception of Immigrants — Preparation of Coloured Artizans and Teachers of Religion for Emigration. Adaptation of African Rivers to Internal Improvements — Relations of the River Niger with Sierra Leone and Liberia, and, through the Chadda, with the Nile — Vast field for Internal Trade and Railroads — Grandeur of the Future of Africa, if properly assisted—The Execution of the Plan would discharge our Debt to the Black Man in full.

THE proposed Board for the management of the Public Domain having been organized, and its powers duly regulated, its first care will necessarily be the preparation of Africa for those who shall be sent there. I do not think that simply transporting men to a new country, with ten, twenty, or more dollars in their pockets to sustain them until they can find employment, is sufficient to secure them against want and disappointment. It is not thus that we can discharge our debt to the negro in a manly and Christian manner. From the very first, efforts should be made to create a demand for labour in Africa. This must be accomplished by aiding the development of African resources in the beginning, by the application of a portion of our own. In a country not overstocked with horses or mules, nothing would seem more natural than that the Liberians should desire the early establishment of railroads. These should therefore receive the prompt attention of the Board.

The very attempt to construct a railroad, would afford the means of living, immediately upon the landing of the immigrant; and, at the same time, it would incite to a high pitch the spirit of improvement in agriculture and building. This would rapidly create other sources of employment — the certainty of employment being better than money in the pocket. The Board should at once turn its attention to the means that would aid the African immigrants in building up their city, and opening their farms as well as their railroads. Consentaneously with these efforts abroad, should be the active employment of such means *here* as would be promotive of colonization. Among the more immediate measures of this class, independent of the encouragement of our iron works, should be the selection of a number of coloured men possessed of the necessary qualifications for making good architects and engineers, and giving them a suitable

G

education, in order to their being sent to Africa for the purpose of giving proper direction to labour upon their public roads and other undertakings. Such practical means as would present themselves for the instruction of negro mechanics, ought to be embraced. The boys of Liberia, as they grow up, ought to be provided with instructors in the mechanical arts. The whole difficulty in this matter lies at the threshold of the movement. Africa, with proper encouragement, would rise in a very few years, through her own energies, to the satisfaction of all her wants in these respects.

Whilst preparations are being made, on the part of the constituted authorities, to qualify Africa for helping herself at home, by sending her such aid as will be physically useful to her, her moral and religious culture should not be left without provision. The former should be well prepared for, by well-regulated schools here; but, as has been already stated, the duty of providing for the latter may be safely confided to the several Christian sects, who cannot be indifferent to the introduction of the gospel on the vast continent whose vital interests we are endeavouring to serve.

The wealthy American man of colour will certainly be strongly induced to emigrate to Africa, as soon as he is satisfied that prompt and permanent measures for the effectual and complete emancipation of his race are about to be adopted; for he has long been sighing for a distinct nationality, being bitterly conscious that *here* no refinement of manners, no wealth, no merit, can elevate him above the social degradation of his race, or place him on an equality with the lowest of ours. When he looks into the future for happiness for his family, his view is lost in doubt: when he seeks for his own, he is disappointed.

How gladly will he embrace Liberia, when she makes sure promise of a home in which he can invest his means, and transact his business in the character of a freeman, while devoting himself to the dignified work of ennobling his long-oppressed country, and his depraved brethren! To him will the necessity of railroads present itself at once, because he practically knows their use. He will either explore the country himself, or send those upon whom he can rely for information, to inquire respecting the soil, climate, rivers, and resources. He will direct his energies to the combination of African gold and African labour in the construction of roads, and the spreading of civilization. He will succeed; for the African has high capacities for industry, let who will deny it, because he does not more strongly display it in the absence of all high and exciting motive.

Let us pause here, for a moment, to glance at the adaptation of African rivers to public improvements. From all the knowledge obtained from maps, travellers, the known course of rivers, and the legitimate deductions drawn from the general forms of contitents and mountain ranges, we have every reason to believe that a railroad could be made from Monrovia to the most important point upon the river Niger, with much less difficulty and far less expense than was attendant upon the making of the Central Railroad from Philadelphia to Pittsburg!

The principal sources of the Niger drain, by a multitude of small streams, a table-land situated not far from the western coast of Africa, between Monrovia and Sierra Leone. This table-land extends over about one degree of latitude, and the various tributaries of this region coalesce into a single great trunk, at the distance of about two hundred miles from each of these centres of African civilization, and at a like distance from the sea. This chief trunk runs in a north-easterly direction, towards the southern edge of the great desert of Zahara, which yields it a few small contributions, and gradually curves it to the south-east and south. Along the most easterly part of its course, it receives tributaries of considerable size from the eastward, some of which interlock with streams supposed to empty into Lake Tchad. From its junction with the largest of them, in about lat. 12° 50″ north, the general course of the Niger is nearly due south, with one easterly bend, to its mouth, in about lat. 4° north; where it falls into the Gulf of Guinea, just east of the Bight of Benin. In about lat. 8° N., long. 7° E., it receives the largest and most important of its branches — the river Chadda or Tchadda — whose tributaries spring from the north side of the mountain range which separates it from the sources of the Congo, and from various widely-separated parts of Central Africa. Of these tributaries, the largest is supposed to be the outlet of the mysterious Lake Tchad; and, by this route, they evidently interlock, either directly, or through the medium of the rivers emptying into that lake, with one of the largest tributaries of the White Nile. In its whole course of more than 2300 miles, the Niger bears a considerable resemblance to a note of interrogation. By the construction of a railroad from Monrovia, to a point on this river near the junction of its early tributaries, the trade of the lesser streams, which are no doubt navigable for small boats, would be made available by the merchants of that young city; and, by continuing this road eastwardly, down the stream to deeper water, at no very great distance, a position would be secured in a highly healthy and fertile region, possessing the same kind of advantages for surrounding trade that Pittsburg presents, at the confluence of the great tributaries of the Ohio river. Here civilization, led on by the American negro pioneer, would penetrate what are generally deemed Central African countries, once powerful, and awaiting but his advent to become so once more. The freedom of access of the civilized negro to these regions, and his influence for good when there, would be infinitely greater than those of the white man. The trade of the eastern tributaries of the Niger would soon be brought to centre at the terminus of the road for the time being, and thus the wealth of a vast interior south of the desert, and extending far beyond Timbuctoo, would be directed towards the Atlantic. At a later day, when free states shall extend eastward along the coast, till they embrace the mouth of the Niger, will be heard the iron steed, snorting on his fiery way along the Chadda, to the sources of the Nile!

The exodus, promoted in the manner I have advocated, will inevitably lead to the populating of the region of the Niger at no distant day. And here, in all probability, will be established the third of the future sisterhood of African free states, founded upon the American model. Imagination conjures up the ghosts of more, like spectres in the glass of Banquo, and loses itself in dreams of the hum of industry, and the "sound of the church-going bell" re-echoed from the "Mountains of the Moon."

Such a state organization once formed in the neighbourhood of a powerful interior kingdom, and in the midst of plains, valleys, and mountain ranges, teeming with intertropical wealth, will the free people of that state imitate the example of our ancestors when they opened to Pittsburg, first a turnpike, then a canal, and finally a railroad? Will they thus progressively and slowly complete their connection with Monrovia? No! They will spring directly to the best refinement of the age — the railroad. They will have within themselves the means to build it, without requiring from us any other aid than tools and iron, after we shall have sent them engineers, carpenters, masons, blacksmiths, and other tradesmen. To judge of the progress of the American negro in Africa by that which has shown itself in the United States, would not be wise; for he will begin at the point we have attained, by the aid of steam, within the last forty years. In this short time we have made more progress than five hundred years would have enabled us to accomplish without it. The American

African will not fall back upon our early progress. Let us suppose that, by any chance, our ancestors had found in the new home of their choice a race of men like our own—their brethren in short— but degraded far below them in civilization. Let us suppose them to have met this race, not as savages against whom it was necessary to raise the dagger in self-defence, but with a grasp of fraternal love and friendship: let us imagine them to have raised this people upon the platform of social equality. Let it be also supposed that, at the same time, they had a knowledge of the power of steam; that they could have induced the natives to useful labour; that they could have received from England iron rails — all the machinery necessary to build steamboats and locomotives, as their sons are now doing — can we doubt that, at this moment, after three hundred years of settlement under such auspices, we should have railroads from the Atlantic to the Pacific Oceans? Can we doubt that Nebraska, and all the country both east and west of the Rocky Mountains, would now be teeming with population, and the land divided into small portions, where

"Every rood of ground maintains its man?"

Will Africa, under circumstances like these, be slow in her progress? Surely not. Her present position, aided in the manner I propose, would be even more favourable to rapidity of progress, than that of our ancestors in the United States, under the circumstances we have supposed.

Long before these improvements are complete, Africa will be prepared safely to receive in large numbers, those children of idle and dissolute coloured parents, who may be unfitted by nature for the task of assisting in the business of the common schools; but these will nevertheless carry away with them a due appreciation of American liberty, and the habits and opinions best calculated to teach a due respect and gratitude for this inestimable blessing, among the benighted and ignorant natives of their unhappy fatherland.

All that I have yet proposed to be done for Africa, is not too much for us to accomplish. We have the means to do it, not only without injury, but with positive advantage to ourselves; and having it in our power to place ourselves in this enviable position, it becomes no less our positive duty than our proper pecuniary policy, to effect the measure. Other moral reasons might be adduced, if necessary, why we should accomplish this urgent purpose. We boast that we are in the enjoyment of privileges, both political and religious, superior to those of any other nation upon earth. We know we have removed, step by step, from the soil on which we have been vouchsafed so many blessings, one race of men, differing in all respects from our own; and that, in so doing, that soil was made to drink their blood. In order to render their destruction more complete, another distinct race of men was brought into requisition. Such facts, however deplorable, have stamped themselves upon our history; yet, in in the face of these facts, we have been favoured beyond measure in all things relating to our social enjoyment and temporal prosperity.

Having attained to a point in national greatness where it becomes politic to be generous, and humane to be just, let us not forget that the price which humanity has paid for the blessings we enjoy has been *the unmitigated slavery of one race of men, and the almost entire destruction of another!* Yes! So completely has the American Indian been removed from our path, that, in a very few years, scarcely one of the race will be left to tell the history of his people, even by way of tradition. Its origin, its mission, its progress, its decay, its fall, in utter desolation and ruin—these will be the themes of many a writer; but where is he, "the monarch of the woods?" Such has been the manifestation of the Divine will; such is the Divine manifestation of that Providence which has suffered a powerful nation to grow up in the short space of less than three hundred years, *standing upon the ruins of one distinct race, and the enslavement of another!*

In carrying forward the great work of the emancipation and redemption of Africa, *charity* claims higher consideration than is often allowed her. Her limits are too often circumscribed by the narrow circle of home. Charity can do much, money can do nothing, morally to compensate the African bondman for the wrongs he has suffered at our hands; for, in his degradation here, we have deprived him of all noble objects of honest ambition. Charity claims that the African should be educated to a full understanding of the principles of our Government, in order that he may become fitted to appreciate the liberty which he has a just right to demand of us, and that he may be thus enabled to teach this liberty to his depraved brethren of another continent, when time and our tardy action shall have placed him where he can do it. In the practice of this liberty, he will have a country as rich as our own, and will no longer want our money. In the practice of such good will to the American African, we shall cancel in full the debt we owe him, by having taught him how to plant kindred institutions in the land of his ancestry.

When we look into the dark vista of African

degradation and African bondage, and find that we can elevate the native African by emancipating the slave, at the small cost of a portion of the proceeds of the now despised Public Domain—improving our own condition, the moral standing, and the prosperity of the nation by this very measure— shall we hesitate to render to the race which has so long and so faithfully served us, the means of unrestrained liberty and national independence?

Let us not even demand colonial vassalage. By so doing, we shall place another gem in the crown of American glory. Shall this thing be done? It can be, if the people will it.

CHAPTER VI.

TENDENCY TO NATIONAL DECAY THROUGH THE INFLUENCE OF SLAVERY.

Interest of the People in Public Affairs, before the Revolution — What corrected the Abuses of those times — Similar Interest in our Early National Days — Enforcement of Law against the Disorderly — Honesty of Government, especially in relation to Public Lands, in successive Administrations, from Washington to Jackson — Commencement of our Rights on Indian Lands by Treaty — Proposal to claim Canada as an Indemnity for the Expenses of the British War — First budding of Pre-emption Laws—First Grants of Land for Internal Improvements and general Economy — Downward Tendency of Public Morals, from the Administration of Monroe to the Present Day, especially with regard to the Public Land Trust, and the Rights of Property and Nations — Large Purchases from the Indians—Loose Extension of the Pre-emption Laws, and its sad Effects — Commercial Expansion—Attempts to check mad Speculations in Lands—Agricultural Madness—Financial Ignorance of Government and People—Apparent Prosperity and Impending Ruin, causes thereof — Collapse of Business — Special Payments suspended— False Views and false Policy—Extravagance, Corruption, and increasing Abuse of the Public Domain — Attempts to extend Slave Territory — Mexican War — Assumption of Debts by Annexation — Presidential Usurpations — Proposal to offer unsold Lands for twenty-five cents per Acre—Millions of Acres squandered — California applies for Admission into the Union — The Slave Question in all its Terrors — Attempts to dissolve the Union — Pre-emption Laws at the Bottom of these Evils — The Free Homestead Bill, to fling away the Patrimony of the People— The Inevitable and Fatal Consequences of our Present Territorial Policy, in Connection with the Permanence of Slavery.

To show how terrible is the curse, how mighty the wrath of God, upon nations that fasten a convulsive grasp upon the slave, I cited the single instance of the bondage of the House of Jacob. I also showed that history proclaims the inevitable desolation of the nations that foster slavery for the indulgence of idleness, profligacy, and licentiousness; and that this institution tends fatally to enervate the powers of a people. I asked the question, whether this nation ought not to come to a pause, and inquire whether or not influences such as have led to the decay of other nations, were not operating upon ourselves. I now mean to show that we have departed from early usages in the administration of the Government, especially in that richest of inheritances, the Public Domain; that the solicitude and watchfulness of the people in relation to the administration of public affairs have declined; and that the institution of slavery lies at the bottom of many of the evils of which the people have just cause to complain, and for which they are loudly called upon to seek a rational remedy.

To contrast our present course of conduct with that of the past, it is not necessary that I should go further back than a few years preceding the Revolutionary War, when the Whigs and Tories — both alike when in power — brought their political actions to bear oppressively upon the interests of the colonies, and, at almost every progressive step, some right was wrested from the people. The power of the Government, through its vast patronage, was then such, that whether Whig or Tory was in the ascendant, even the election of new men to office did not change the current of oppression. The patriot stood appalled at the constant succession of new acts on the part of the King and the Colonial Legislatures, which wrested from him personal rights and rights of property, with a rapidity that threatened to impoverish him, and enslave his posterity. Have we not, in the progress of less than one century of independence, reached a point when it becomes obvious that the selfish ends of politicians are as destructive of national economy and the rights of the citizen as was the political power exercised by George III. and the Colonial Legislatures?

In those colonial times, new men were frequently elected to the Legislature. Governors who had rendered themselves obnoxious to popular censure were also frequently removed from office, and new men appointed, with a promise that such measures as were thought calculated to destroy the liberties of the people, and such as the people most bitterly complained of, should be repealed. Although new rulers were placed in authority, those objectionable laws were seldom repealed. On the contrary, the evils complained of, were fastened upon the people with aggravated force. The patriot of former times, in the workings of his own isolated thoughts, would continually exclaim, "How can these extortions and oppressions for the promotion of the selfish ends of the politician be arrested?" In these patriots, (few in number at the time when the first approaches of despotism were perceived,) was highly concentrated that far-sighted love of country which diffused itself in a greater or lesser degree through the minds of all the colonists, except such as looked with a more than prudent regard to the power and influence wealth would yield them, under the prostrating influence of colonial vassalage.

But the office-holder and the politician found their interests secured by a close adherence to the power of the British crown; because the patronage of the crown was daily augmented by a policy which brought the people into a direct and dangerous dependence upon the parent Government. The man of peace, and the prudent man, who regarded his own safety and that of his family, more than anything else—together with such as are ever found with the majority, caring not for right or wrong, provided they may win the smile of power—were readily induced to strengthen oppression by a servile vote. The true patriot, as he stood isolated amidst this powerful array of selfishness, in deep solicitude for his country, was forced to exclaim, "Alas! I am but a single man!" In a hope so forlorn as this, men began to communicate their sentiments to each other in the most guarded manner. They knew not that the feeling for the honour and glory of their country so deeply concentrated in themselves, consuming their hearts through anxious days and sleepless nights, was broadly scattered throughout the land, and was working, with greater or less force, in the minds of thousands, so as to fit each for his proper sphere of action in a great struggle for the overthrow of the sordid and selfish politician, and the elevation of his country to national independence.

Yes, my countrymen! When the burning lights that shone through the lowering clouds and the deep gloom of our political morning, brightening with hope the trial-beset path that led to the temple of Liberty;—when the brightest and purest first met within the circle of their firesides, to speak of the wrongs heaped upon their country;— the first promulgation of the idea of independence startled them to their feet; where, in all their manhood, they stood appalled at the temerity of the speaker, feeling the halter already around their necks! Upon retaking their seats, seeing the political party influences by which they were surrounded, all tending to rivet the chains of vassalage, and secure the desolation of their country, they asked, in their well-grounded fear, " Are we a Sodom or Gomorrah? Can ten patriots be found to save the colonies?" Such was the terror that then suppressed the free expressions of patriotism throughout the land! The small assemblages gathered around the fireside to escape intrusion were not known to each other. But, as oppression assumed a more open and determined aspect, in the display of wealth and prodigality by the subservient politician at home, and the despotism of king and parliament abroad, these fireside patriots, by an affinity that naturally drew them together, became known to each other. The community of sentiment which this proximity revealed was soon found to be *national*. The fireside discussion of national wrongs then ceased to be dreaded, as involving the question of personal treason. If treason to the constituted authorities was embraced in such debates, it was a *national* treason.

From this moment, the wrongs done by the Government were proclaimed by the people everywhere; the means of redress, and the propriety of such means, were carefully examined; appeals to the governing powers, of the strongest and most urgent character, emanated from the public meetings, setting forth the evil operation upon themselves, and the pernicious influence upon posterity, of the oppressive laws so strongly contended for by the Government. At this moment of trial, when they were obliged to meet the hostility of Great Britain, exerted through her vast and subduing patronage, extending itself widely over the world, and especially throughout the colonies, they foresaw the enervating and deadening influence that the public spoils would exert upon the purely selfish. They saw that, by means of such, the debased in spirit and selfish in purpose would be induced to support the Government to the last. They knew that the politician, in the maintenance of a bad cause, would leave nothing untried, however disgraceful, to influence the timid and cautious, who are generally as selfish in private gains as the demagogue is in public spoils or plunder. They knew, too, that such combined influences as these would operate upon all classes of men, with a force that must render their final success doubtful in the minds of many. With all these disheartening circumstances operating against them, but with a full conviction that they were right in their demands, truthful in their charges of wrong, and patriotic in the effort to secure the independence of their country, they marched rapidly forward, in defiance of daily increasing encroachments, till the time arrived when fifty-six of the noblest spirits of the day were delegated to form, for the oppressed colonies, a committee of safety known and designated as the Continental Congress.

These delegates, branded by the Tory who lived on the spoils of his country, as traitors, pledged "their lives, their fortunes, and their sacred honour" to the independence of their country. Traitors? No! This Congress united nearly the unanimous voice of a nation seeking its future independence through a course of the severest trials, heaped upon it by the despotism of the few! No disasters, however great, discouraged them; nor did the patriotic army, with its noble chief at its head, shrink from the accomplishment of its purpose, though the line of its marches might be traced by the blood poured from the shoeless foot of the soldier. *Our independence was achieved*, through poverty and toil and discouraging disasters, by men inspired with a patriotic hope that the pains and blood it cost would be regarded as the price of its future benefits, and a security for the maintenance of equal rights to the citizens of the confederated colonies.

This Congress, after independence was accomplished, soon found itself involved in serious difficulty, in directing the government of a country embracing a great variety of soil, climate, and interests, in consequence of its not having been endowed with any specific power to regulate those interests for the equitable advantage of the whole territory. This important defect was taken into consideration by the people, in public meetings throughout the confederation; and the means by which the conflicting rights of the various sections could be equitably adjusted, were fully discussed; so also were all the measures which led to the declaration of independence; and the Constitution became *as direct a result of the immediate action of the people* as was the Revolutionary War.

The Administration, during the first eight years of this constitution, was obliged, in every measure which it adopted, to look carefully forward into the progress of time, to see what would be its bearing on the future. The establishment of an army and navy was looked upon as necessary, to meet, in time of need, those urgent demands which are made upon every people when compelled to resist the aggressions of other nations, even when the means of defence are ample. But when the Father of his Country retired from the presidential chair, his solicitude for the future interests of his country was so deep, and his heartfelt anxiety so warm, that he could not retire without the expression of his feelings in a farewell address, through the Congress of the United

States, to the whole people. How faithfully the cautions and advice in this fatherly address have been regarded, we shall see.

The administration of John Adams increased the naval force of the United States, and augmented that of the army. In the most formidable war we ever had with the Indians — that in which Gen. St. Clair was defeated, and which Gen. Wayne brought to a close in the year 1795 — the Indians were so completely subdued as to secure to the United States, by treaty, the right to station upon Indian territory any portion of the American army which the Government might order there, for the protection of the country and the aborigines. This right was exercised, and portions of our army were so stationed at Forts Recovery, St. Mary, Brown, Finley, Meigs, Defiance, Wayne, and other points. But peace being fully established, the necessity and propriety of this increase of the army was denied in Congress, and by many of the leading newspapers in the country.

A new and experimental government, looking to the interests of thirteen sovereign states and the future settlement of a Public Domain, was necessarily required to provide for vast expenses in defending and protecting that Domain against the Indians. The accomplishment of this duty demanded more money than the Government could secure from the revenues arising from commerce, and some system of taxation became indispensable, in aid of the ordinary income. For this purpose, a direct tax, an excise, and stamp act were enacted. In addition to these, an alien law was passed, requiring of the foreigner a residence of fourteen years in the country before becoming entitled to citizenship. Portions of these tax laws soon became obnoxious to complaint; especially the law laying an excise upon whiskey; and in Pennsylvania this law was resisted. The Father of his Country, who had been for some time in the well-deserved enjoyment of the ease afforded to a private citizen after retiring from his vast public trusts, was prompt in his exertions to secure the proper execution of the laws. He accepted the offer of commander-in-chief, and marched at the head of an army to put down the whiskey insurrection. To enforce the collection of taxes, and respect for the laws and the Government, a sedition law was also passed. This law was an error on the part of the Government. It had more effect in defeating and changing the Administration, than all the others combined, though popular clamour endeavoured to render them all odious alike.

The Administration was everywhere assailed.

Liberty poles were erected in many parts of the country; the cutting down of which, and the arrest of some persons who were active in raising them, led to so complete an organization of the Democratic party, as to enable it to elect Thomas Jefferson to the Presidency, by a small majority, in the year 1800. The administration of John Adams was long pointed at as the reign of terror; and the demagogue, even now, to secure popular clamour against a candidate for office, will cry out — " Federalist!"

All matters, *pro* and *con*, connected with this administration, were discussed with such scrutinizing pertinacity, that a schoolboy who could read the newspapers could not fail to understand the merits of the questions at issue. No measure affecting the constitutional rights of the citizen could fail, in those days, to elicit a close examination by the whole people, not only with a view to its present bearing, but its future tendencies also. This " Vigilence is the price of Liberty;" yet it will be seen how little we now regard enormities vastly more pernicious in their consequences than anything that occurred during the administration of John Adams, except the sedition law.

But, I say, let every Administration do as did that of John Adams, in patriotically standing up for the execution of laws, against all popular clamour, until they are repealed. Let the people, as they did formerly, break down measures which they may be obliged, at a later day, to re-establish — as in the case of our defensive policy; but let them, at least, discuss and agitate all measures, until they comprehend them! Any action is better than indifference and the tame resignation of the liberty, honour, and independence of the country, into the hands of irresponsible politicians! Thus, and thus only, we can escape the censure of posterity for a faithless, slothful neglect of the lessons of our ancestors, and the high hope of the nation.

Thomas Jefferson, in his administration, yielded by necessity to the unpopularity of the army and navy with the party then dominant. He was obliged to reduce the army to such a degree, as to render it incapable of protecting the lives of the frontier settlers against murder and devastation, in case of another Indian war. The Federalists, who saw deeper into the future interests and necessities of the country than their political antagonists, were compelled to witness with sorrow the laying up of nearly the whole navy, and the refusal to build more vessels, in despite of all the appeals they could make to change this course of policy; this party being in the minority. For the protection of commerce, a gun-boat system was established, which proved to be so very inefficient, that England, being in want of seamen while engaged in a war with France, and seeing the United States without adequate means of defence upon the element of which she claimed to be the mistress, trampled, with the greatest audacity, upon both our trade and our personal rights. She impressed our seamen with impunity. But, whatever was done to resist the aggression of the British upon our commerce and our personal rights, was regularly laid before Congress according to law; and, in 1807, an embargo was laid, as being calculated to deter the British from the impressment of our citizens into their service. This measure was enforced for only a very short time — not more than sixty days. It proved to be unpopular, and was not re-enacted.

James Madison succeeded to the Presidency in March, 1809; and, during his administration, a Non-intercourse Act was passed, in the hope of inducing Great Britain to respect the rights of our citizens—this country being then very indifferently prepared for war. War, however, was declared in 1812, and continued upon land, lake, and sea, until the final battle was fought at New Orleans in 1815; in which battle this nation achieved one of the most bloodless victories on our part, when the result is compared with the loss of the enemy, that can be found upon record.

But that which, in the history of this war, I conceive to be of the greatest importance to my present argument with the people is, that every subject in connection with it was discussed by the people themselves. Its causes and its aims were thoroughly understood. The country felt that it was based upon the rights of the American citizen; and, for the maintenance of those rights, the people, like their ancestors, were then willing to peril all. But in the management of the negotiation for peace, by commissioners appointed by the President and the Senate, the selection of the men, the orders of the commissioners, their place of meeting with the British, and their whole proceedings during the negotiation, *were laid before the people.* Everything in connection with the terms of treaty was known to all the citizens; and *all* discussed the preliminaries of the treaty, and the claims based thereon, without disguise. It was then maintained by some few, that, on just principles, the Canadas ought to be claimed as an indemnity for the expenses of the war; but the Government decided that the war was never intended to promote the acquisition of territory, and all that it claimed, all that the nation could in honour ask, had been achieved. This conclusion met the cordial approbation of the people; and the preliminaries of the treaty embraced no territory beyond the boundaries of the nation, as they existed before the war. Peace was declared throughout the country in the winter of 1815, a very few days' after the battle of New Orleans.

The expenditures of the war had embarrassed the finances of the country in such a way as to render it expedient that the Government should charter a Bank of the United States; and the same Administration that refused to re-charter the old "Federal Bank of the United States," now chartered one with a capital more than three times as great as that of the old Bank!

The Federalists, being the only party in opposition to the Democratic party up to this time, made feeble opposition to the first election of James Monroe. They had seen all that they had built up, as in their belief conducive to the interests of the country, pulled down, and again built up by the Democratic party! So, having nothing left to contend for in point of principle, and not choosing to exert what might appear to be a mere factious hostility towards this incumbent, they suffered the second election of this statesman to go by default, and it was nearly unanimous. The people sank down into a calm in relation to political matters, the like of which they had not experienced within the preceding sixty years. But notwithstanding the quietude of this Administration, it was conducted upon the strictest principles of economy; the national debt, which was caused by the war, was rapidly paid off; the land system was perfected in a way to secure to each citizen his right in the Public Domain; free gifts and pre-emption rights were guarded with the utmost care; so that, in 1820, when pre-emptions were asked for in aid of canals and county-seats, one-quarter section was granted to each new county in the state of Ohio, for the purpose of erecting county buildings thereon. In the year 1822, ninety feet in width of land only was granted to the Illinois canal, connecting the Illinois river with Lake Michigan. In the year 1824, a similar grant was made to the state of Indiana, to connect the waters of the Wabash river with Lake Erie. In the canvass for a President in the autumn of 1824, William H. Crawford, John Quincy Adams, Henry Clay, and Andrew Jackson were all presented as candidates. Neither of these having received a majority of electoral votes, the election of President came constitutionally before Congress. John Quincy Adams was chosen; and, upon his election, a violent party opposition sprang up, and the Administration was assailed from the first moment of its existence. Indeed, the charge of corruption by bargain was at once asserted by Gen. Jackson himself, he having had a plurality of electoral votes. This Administration was charged with the practice of corruptions of the deepest cast in connection with the "Federal" bank of the United States; with unbounded extravagance *in furnishing the "East Room" of the President's House;* and, with other matters, faults connected with the expenditures of the public money on the part of the Government. On all sides, Gen. Jackson's heroism, virtue, and patriotism were extolled to the skies; and such a popular clamour was raised throughout the country, that everything gave way before it. The day came when the "Augean stable was to be cleansed," and Gen. Jackson was elected President of the United States. When the smoke by which the administration of John Quincy Adams had been enveloped throughout its whole career was blown away, it was found that the expenditures of public money exceeded by a very little that of the preceding Administration! It was shown that the National Debt had been so rapidly diminished, that, by the continuance of the same prudence and economy which had been observed during the four years of this dynasty, the National Debt would be liquidated within the succeeding four years. This necessary result followed during the Presidency of Gen. Jackson.

It was proclaimed that the National Debt was extinguished, and popular clamour attributed to the hero of New Orleans the policy by which this great end was accomplished. It was found that the transactions of the Government under Adams with the Bank of the United States, were of a strictly legal character, and that the "East Room," if furnished at all, was the reverse of extravagant in its dress and appearance. When the historian shall travel over the period of time at which I have only glanced, he will justly credit this Administration with having possessed as much purity of purpose, and with being controlled by as noble a spirit of patriotism as any that preceded it.

In this very general outline of the history of past events, my object is to show that the action of the Government, and that of the people, notwithstanding the political calm that prevailed throughout the administration of James Monroe, was at all times calculated to promote the high advancement of the country, and maintain a full and perfect respect for the equal rights of property and persons; that the difference of opinion between the Federal and Democratic parties related only to the proper application of means to elevate the prosperity, happiness, honour, and worthy distinction of the nation; and that the continued pursuit of such a policy would have secured, to this hour, the just and equitable rights of the people, especially in the proceeds of the Public Domain; while, by contrasting the corrupt and selfish conduct of the politician of succeeding Administrations with the patriotism of the past, I shall proceed to show how totally, and how fatally, that policy has been changed.

In the year 1827, a law was passed granting to the state of Illinois a strip of land extending along the line of the contemplated Illinois canal, to the distance of *five miles* on each side of this work, reserving each alternate section. A similar grant was also made in favour of the Wabash and Erie canal. These laws were urged upon the plea that, as the New York canal was completed to the city of Buffalo, the sooner canals were made to extend into the wilderness, from the upper end of Lake Erie, the better; for, that the effect of these improvements would be, to enhance the value of the remaining Government lands so greatly, that they would produce more money than the whole Domain in the absence of such necessary works. This was the first step made by Congress in granting land for purposes of internal improvement. In the year 1828, the Indian title to a tract of land generally known as the St. Joseph's Purchase, was extinguished. This tract extended from the most southern bend of Lake

Michigan, in the state of Indiana, northward into the state of Michigan, and thence, eastward, to the Ohio state line. This land was of high value, being fine woodland, interspersed with prairie.

The administration of Gen. Jackson went into operation in March, 1829. This Administration brought together the ultra Federalist and the aspiring Democrat, and in a common cause made friends of personal enemies. The "Augean stable was to be cleansed," and to do this, men heretofore holding the most opposite opinions united in this patriotic task. In the first year of this Administration, although pre-emption rights for lands had been previously granted only with the utmost caution, and never to any great extent, a pre-emption law was passed, covering the prairie lands in the tract just mentioned. In the year 1832, a vast body of land lying north and west of the Wabash and Eel rivers, was purchased from the Pottawattamie Indians. The pre-emption right was extended to this land also. The treaty by which it was acquired differed from all preceding Indian treaties, in providing for certain "reserves," in terms calculated to hold out inducements for the largest private speculations, of the nature of direct frauds upon the Government; and from this time forward, throughout this Administration, the pre-emption laws were extended to all purchases of land from the Indians. This system laid the basis of one of the most widely-extended and wildest land speculations ever known in the country, carried out by men alike regardless of private rights and the rights of the Government: it unhinged every department of business in the country. The means of access to this portion of the Public Domain was made easy through the New York canal and the Lakes. In the year 1835, it was stated to me that Laporte county, Indiana, had a population of 10,000 inhabitants, though the first cabin was built in the county only four years before. Chicago, where the first house was built in 1831, had its thousands of inhabitants in 1835. Logansport then contained 1000 inhabitants, though the first edifice was constructed in 1832; and many other villages were found to have grown with like rapidity. The excessive rapidity of emigration into this country, together with the fact that every emigrant, even though an agriculturalist by profession, was a *consumer* for eighteen months before he could, by his own exertion, secure the means of living for himself and family, caused the prices of flour and everything else to rise higher in this new settlement than in the city of New York; so that we can fairly account for the importation of breadstuffs into this country, to fill up the vacuum caused by the consumption in the interior, in the years 1834, '35, and '36 — though it should be the chief granary of the world. Nor were land speculations by any means confined to this spot: they were extended over the whole Public Domain.

This mania for dealing in new lands, to the prejudice of the manufacturing and other leading departments of business, was stimulated into the greatest activity by the forcible transfer of the public deposits from the United States Bank to the state banks; so that more of the public lands were sold in five years after the removal of these deposits, than had been taken up from the year 1796 to 1833!—without having elicited upon the part of the people any close examination into the cause of this morbid excitement. It produced intoxication in commercial pursuits, and a feverish excitement in agriculture. It encouraged idleness in the adventurer, and stimulated the capitalist and dashing speculator into a recklessness of consequences, for which no parallel can be found, except in the equally reckless administration of the Government.

If a prudent regard for the true principles which should regulate the monetary operations of a country had marked the management of the national finances, instead of the war which was waged upon the Bank of the United States, to the destruction of the comforts of the aged, the widow, and the orphan; if, instead of placing the money within the grasp of speculating office-holders, the proceeds of the Public Domain had been administered with justice towards both the Government and the people, and in a manner consistent with the terms of the trust and the dictates of sound morals, we should not have had a suspension of specie payments almost on the same day that this Administration drew to a close.

The operations upon the Public Domain in the years 1835 and 1836 became so extravagant, that the President of the United States attempted a partial check by issuing the specie circular, as it was called. This circular, or order from the Executive, required all lands to be sold for gold or silver, except that three hundred and twenty acres might be sold to any actual settler, payable in notes of a deposit bank; all other revenues being payable in notes of these banks. This circular, like the removal of the deposits from the United States Bank, was proclaimed by popular clamour as an instance of the iron nerve of the President, and a proof that his course was governed by the love of country. Yes! it was reiterated on all sides, that the patriotism of "the old hero" was so staunch, and his firmness so unshaken, that all dishonest men in place, all land and bank speculators, would be arrested in their course of obvious plunder. In such a light did the morbid devotion of the people to the hero of New Orleans induce them to view, through the fog raised by corrupt politicians, the patriotism of the President, at the very moment when he had permitted agriculture, the grand and leading interest of the country, to run into the wildest disorder, fomenting that disorder by his favourite measures! Old farms were abandoned, and new ones sought upon the Public Domain. The mere loss of time to this interest from an emigration which obliged each emigrant to purchase his means of living for eighteen months, before his labours could be made productive, was the source of incalculable loss to this great interest. State stocks issued by the old states for constructing internal improvements, which alone rendered the public lands of such value as caused them to be grasped at with the ferocity of the tiger, were perverted into the means for increasing the importation of iron and breadstuffs, by which commerce was inordinately inflated, and every department of business was thrown into a confusion such as boys often delight in creating, utterly forgetful of their want of power to correct the mischiefs they are recklessly perpetrating.

By way of comparison, I would illustrate the

effects of Gen. Jackson's administration by supposing a large number of persons placed in a room heated by a furnace; the temperature of the room, the furniture, &c., being in most proper order when they enter it; and the orders to the stokers of the furnace being such that, if not understood by the guests, they must cause the apartment to be overheated to a dangerous degree. In our case, the cause of the heat, lying at a distance from the room, did not evidently manifest itself to the party within; a difference of opinion existed as to the cause of the undue temperature, and each maintained his theory with regard to it. But, none understanding the truth, the heat continued to operate with increased force, all the while, until there was imminent danger that the house would be burned to the ground. Meanwhile, the real cause of the mischief was simply this:—*the stokers were constantly adding more fuel to the fire in the furnace below!*

The Hero President retired from office, leaving an address of advice to the people, recommending patriotic motives for their guidance, and promising, by such means, the long continuance of such national prosperity as existed at the time. But alas for human vanity! His successor was obliged, in the short space of a few weeks, to call an extra Congress, to take into consideration the embarrassment into which the monetary interests of the country were thrown! This Congress met in the month of September following the inauguration of Martin Van Buren as President of the United States, (one of the persons who had been in the heated room, but has not yet been found willing publicly to acknowledge the true cause of the heat, if he has ever been able to detect it). In his message to this Congress, he says, " The history of trade in the United States for the last three years, affords the most convincing evidences that our present condition is chiefly to be attributed to over action in all the departments of business; an over action deriving, perhaps, its first impulses from antecedent causes, but stimulated to its destructive consequences by excessive issues of bank paper, and by other facilities for the acquisition and enlargement of credit."

That "over-action" should be produced by antecedent causes, which causes themselves consisted in "over-action," is not good logic. It is *over-action producing over-action*. And that this over-action should be stimulated by effects growing out of over-action, is still worse; for, the principles by which bank-issues are governed would no more permit this result than they would enable them to remedy the result when produced. The truth is, that banks may *contract* their business at pleasure; but an antecedent cause must exist, to enable them to *expand!* Had the President referred to the necessities of the immigrant upon the public lands; to the over-action in selling which he was invited to by pre-emption laws;—had he referred also to the demands created by the building of steamboats, canal-boats, and every other appliance for the accommodation of this vast immigration; to state credits inflating commerce by the importation of breadstuffs, and iron, and silks in excess; then, to the demands that the public works in progress at the time created;—had he given attention to the really steady and prudent operation of the United States Bank—directing his glance rather to the interests of its stockholders than to the demands of rapacious politicians;—and had he given a due consideration to the argument used in connection with the removal of the deposits; namely: that "now state banks could supply the wants of the people"—he would have shown, in the plainest possible manner, how bank facilities were demanded by the antecedent causes created by the Government, in driving the leading departments of business into morbid action, in a false direction!

In the first annual message of the President to Congress, (he still not understanding the causes of disaster to the country; and the speculations in land still running high, notwithstanding the suspension of specie payments;) it was recommended that the prices of land should be graduated; a lower price being asked for such as had been in the market for fifteen years, and still remained unsold. Doubtless, every politician and land speculator connected with the Government understood the plausible fallacy of this suggestion. In fact, if the recommendation had been carried into effect, it would have facilitated the winning of the largest kind of profits by the speculator; for the following reasons: —

I have said that strips of land five miles in width along each side of the Wabash and Erie, and Miami canals had been granted to these canals. Now, when the plan of graduation was proposed, the strips next adjoining these belts, extending in length one hundred miles upon the former, and seventy on the latter, and altogether amounting to millions of acres, had already been in market fifteen years! These canals have their course along the Maumee and Auglaize rivers. The five mile grants upon each side of these were, of course, taken out of market in order to obtain for them the highest price when the canals should be completed; this being the only way to make them properly available for meeting the expenses of construction; and some of these lands were ultimately sold for more than twenty dollars per acre. Meanwhile, the belts on either side of the five mile tracts, thus reserved, remained unsold, because those river-belt lands were not in the market; such lands, for many reasons, being always taken up first in a new country. But any canal, at a distance of eight hundred miles from the city of New York, confers increased value on all adjoining lands, to the distance of ten, twenty, or even thirty miles. Had the proposition of the Executive been carried out, the unsettled belts, though soon to be enormously enhanced in value, would have been made purchasable at mere nominal prices, and would have been picked up by great speculators, (who could afford to await the settlement of the country,) at twenty-five or fifty cents per acre! Besides; there were other millions of unsettled acres in the Domain that, at that time, had already been in market for fifteen years, and unsold, not because they were less fertile than other lands, but simply for the reason that "Indian reserves" and other natural causes retarded their settlement. It is obvious that, just to the degree that the proposed arrangement would have enriched the mere speculator, at the future expense of the settler, it would have tended to impoverish the Government. Under the unwise if not dishonest policy which has been now sketched out, by the time this Administration drew to a close, the disasters which it and its immediate predecessor had brought on the country, had sunk state and other credits, and business of all kinds, to the most depressed condition. The yearly expenditures of the Jackson and Van Buren dynasties rose from $14,000,000 (the amount in John Quincy Adams's administration,) to $20,000,000, $30,000,000, and even as high as $40,000,000!

The people were now made to feel that public affairs had been mismanaged. "Tippecanoe and Tyler too," together with log cabins and barrels of hard cider, were brought by another popular clamour into the election canvass. Gen. William Henry Harrison was elected President, but died shortly after his inauguration; and John Tyler, by the right of his election as Vice-President, became President of the United States.

The active business of the country had been prostrated in the dust. Speculations of all kinds had apparently ceased. But, did this state of things determine the new set of politicians introduced into the administration, to carry out such reforms as would be calculated to bring back the course of Government to the standard which it maintained from the beginning, up to the time of the election of Jackson? No evidence of such an intention was made to appear. The passage of a tariff law seemed to have the effect of reviving the business of the country, but the rapacity of the politician for the spoils of office, (as the public funds were still regarded,) continued, to all seeming, as grasping and uncompromising as it had been during the two preceding Administrations. No reforms in the expenditure of money were effected. What most distinguished the new dynasty was, that it took measures to bring the state of Texas into the Union, on its own prompting, and when the majority of the people had neither examined into the necessity of annexation, nor desired it. This whole matter was arranged for the people by Texan bond-holders and slave-holders, for the joint, but exclusive benefit of both. To bondholders, annexation on condition that the United States should assume the Texan indebtedness, was of the highest importance. The debt of Texas amounted to several millions of dollars. The bonds had been sold in the market for much less than par value. The speculators in these bonds secured vast fortunes by annexation. But that which seemed to cause the most bitter feeling against the measure was, that it increased the number of slave states. Public land speculations produced little or no excitement during this Administration.

When President Tyler retired from office, James

K. Polk was inaugurated. The people chose him in preference to Henry Clay, notwithstanding that he had taken a conspicuous part, during the administration of Gen. Jackson, in the support of measures that had a tendency to prostrate the credit of the country. This Administration soon adopted measures by which it might draw as largely upon the public purse as its predecessors had done. It seemed as if the principle that "to the victors belong the spoils," was destined to be maintained as fully in force as when it was first proclaimed. Change of parties in the Government had no tendency to produce reform of abuses. As one or the other of the political factions of the day obtained the ascendency, it seemed only necessary to repeal a tariff, or advance some other mere *measure* that was contended for as a *principle*, in the electioneering canvass. This Administration determined upon a war with Mexico, and absolutely brought it about in a manner without precedent at any previous period during the existence of this Government.

The first fact that forces itself on our attention in connection with this war is, that Mexico owed the United States some millions of dollars, the payment of which had been urged, on the part of the United States, for several years. Mexico, in the meantime, was reduced to bankruptcy by internal dissension and strife; so that she was too poor to make payment, and too weak to resist the power which the Administration was able to bring to bear in order to subdue her. Political jealousies also rendered her armies unreliable; and such was her whole condition, that she presented an easy conquest. Had the California gold been known to her, doubtless the pretence of the war would have been removed.

Another and most important point in relation to this war presents itself; which is, that the President concentrated the army upon the Rio Grande while Congress was actually in session, without making known to that body the disposition he was making of the army, or the fact that Mexico, seeing the warlike demonstration, was also marching her forces towards her frontier, to resist the invasion of her territory, if such was contemplated. These armies met in hostile array; and then only was Congress called upon to declare war against Mexico, and vote appropriations to carry this war forward, chiefly upon the plea of indemnity.

Could James Madison have concentrated the American army upon the frontiers of Canada, and involved the people in a war with England upon so slight a pretence? No; he could not have done it! The debasing influence of Government patronage was not felt or known to the Congress of 1812. It required the full force of this influence, brought to bear upon the politician, to induce an almost unanimous submission to the will of the Dictator of this war! FOURTEEN PATRIOTS voted against the appropriation. The spirit that induced this vote finds an echo in the hearts of a large class of American citizens; but, under the reign of partisan politicians, this class is as powerless to accomplish a reform of abuses, now and here, as were the patriots who lived in the period just prior to the Revolutionary War, to resist the encroachments of British oppression, while communion of sentiment was unknown to exist among them. But when this union of sentiment was discovered to our forefathers of those trying times, the patronage of the Government, and the selfishness of the politician had to yield, and give place to the might and majesty of the people. Nor will the daily wrongs that Congress commits against the people cease, until the people shall determine that the rights of states and the equal rights of all, *shall* be respected. Before the Revolutionary War, and during that fearful and bloody struggle, the conflict between the citizen contending for his equal rights, and the despotism of the office-holder, was terrible even to contemplate; but, to secure the equal rights of all *now*, nothing more than a proper use of the ballot-box is necessary.

A third fact is; that, upon the conclusion of this war, no indemnity was claimed for the five millions which Mexico owed us, nor for the seventy or eighty millions the war cost us; nor for the vast treasure of American blood that crimsoned the soil of Mexico. All! all was waived for the acquisition of territory! Nor was even this an indemnity; for, at least as much money was paid for this territory as would have purchased it without a war!

The treaty by which peace was restored was secured by a private agent of the President, under instructions dictated by him, independently of Congress, and was as suddenly sprung upon the Senate for ratification, as the necessity for money to carry on the war had been upon the House of Representatives.

How very progressive is modern Democracy! But, upon what plea, other than a gross assumption derogatory to the people, if not destructive of their rights, could the Executive make a purchase of territory, or enforce a war of any kind, without the knowledge of Congress?

I tell you, my countrymen, that when a President of the United States can determine war or peace on the principle of a mere dictator, with no fear of any higher authority,—no dread of the majesty of the people, acting through their constitutional agents,—

but, by the mere force of Government patronage — the time has come when you ought to inquire what are the influences that sustain so great a wrong to yourselves as has been the Mexican war!

The motives which induced the perpetration of this wrong, the future will reveal. If the purposes were the extension of slavery into California, that object has been signally defeated by the discovery of gold. But, however much this discovery may have disappointed the slave interest, yet it is the only salve that covers the festering sores of this national "fillibustering."

This Administration could not resist the temptation to continue, and endeavour to increase the abuses in the management of the public lands. It suggested that, if those lands which had been in market a given number of years, should be reduced to *twenty-five cents per acre*, a large sum of money would be secured to meet the expenses of the war; thus making evil the parent of evil.

I cannot resist the temptation to enlarge a little here on the effects which would be produced by the plans of graduation in the price of public lands, whether that suggested by Martin Van Buren, or that of James K. Polk, who proposed to fix the minimum at twenty-five cents per acre.

At the time when this graduation was first proposed; that is, during the Presidency of Martin Van Buren; the lands that had been in market for fifteen years and still remained unsold, were those adjoining the five-mile strips of canal grants, which have been alluded to in the foregoing pages, together with a vast number of acres adjoining Indian reserves in the states of Ohio and Indiana. The whole country in the immediate neighbourhood of these reserves had become settled, except a belt around each, some five or six miles in width, which was left unoccupied; few persons being willing to submit to a closer proximity to the Indians, although negotiations for their removal were actually in progress at the time. The lands surrounding the reserves, and lying at a distance from them, were readily bought at one dollar and twenty-five cents per acre; yet they were of the same character with those which were to be brought under the graduated price. Of course, it is obvious how the speculator would profit by such a law. It now requires $125,000 to buy 100,000 acres; but under the proposed new law, this sum would buy half a million of acres.

When the reserves were brought into market a few years afterwards, the land sold, in many instances, for more than ten dollars per acre! Of course, those nearest the settlements were held to be of higher value. The lands that, at this present time, have been in market for fifteen years and more, and which are therefore treated as worthless by the designing, are really of as great or still greater value; as is proved by the recent history of the swamp lands given to the states in which they lie. These swamp lands may be considered as among the best in the country; especially those in the states of Michigan, Indiana, Illinois, Iowa, Wisconsin, and Missouri. These are among the richest grass lands of the West. When drained, which in most instances can readily be done, they constitute the most productive corn lands in the Domain; and when the country shall be fully settled, (and it is rapidly approaching this condition,) these will possess double the value of any others in their vicinity. Many of these tracts have indeed a soil so rich in mould, in consequence of the decay of their annual product of vegetable matter, that the earth itself will prove, in the course of time, an invaluable manure for the land immediately surrounding them! These swamps or unappreciated tracts are generally found upon what may be called the table-land ; except where, as sometimes happens, they occur at the confluence of streams, or where, as is frequently the case, they lie along the course of streams, like the marshes ordinarily found on the margins of rivers emptying into the ocean. The reader is aware that such marshes are now among the most highly-prized grounds in the country.

The table-land of which I speak divides the waters of the Lakes from those of the Mississippi river. This region is very extensive; and, as the smallest streams generally take their rise in a swamp, the land capable of being thus redeemed amounts to millions of acres! The swamps upon this vast table-land are of all sizes, from a few acres up to 150,000 acres. The smaller swamps — those containing 1000 or even 2000 acres, or less — when found in the settled portion of the Domain, are generally bought up by the farmers who have established themselves around them; each being anxious to secure a portion of such valuable meadow and pasture ground for the benefit of his upland. But where swamps are much larger, the settlers have heretofore purchased mainly on their edges; and the settlements around them enjoy, at present, all the advantages of hay and pasture ground, without being obliged to purchase it; because, until a joint effort at drainage is made by the neighbours, or until some public aid is extended for this purpose, these wet tracts are not considered purchasable. But ways and means may be readily found to blow away ledges of rocks crossing the streams which are the outlets of the swamps, and then these lands will be found to rise enormously in value.

As has been already hinted, all these rich tracts have been unconditionally granted by Congress to the several states in which they lie. I feel but little disposition to complain of this appropriation, which, at least, secures their real value to the public, instead of squandering it upon private speculators, though it would be difficult to explain on correct moral grounds, the action of Congress in the case, when viewed as the *common trustee of all the states*, under the original deeds of cession. The extent of the donation may be guessed at from the fact that some of these swamp lands, all of which it was proposed to sacrifice at twenty-five cents per acre, have since been actually sold at *fifty dollars per acre;* nor is it at all improbable that other lands may hereafter lie unsold on the market for fifteen years, though likely, in a few years more, to be enhanced two hundred per cent. in value. Many tracts are so circumstanced at present.

Many persons suppose that it is necessary to go to the Land Office within the district, in order to purchase Government lands. This is a great mistake; and, to remove the impression, I will narrate a queer occurrence that took place in the City of Washington, during Gen. Jackson's administration.

While one set of the friends of that President were extolling him throughout the country for his stern patriotism in directing the issue of his Special Circular, another set of his friends were at Washington, buying lands in large quantities *with one single keg of specie!* The way it was done was this: — one set of speculators borrowed the specie and bought land: the Land Office deposited the keg in the bank. Another set then re-borrowed it, and purchased more land; and, in this way, the keg was carried from the bank to the Land Office, and back, at each transit virtually embezzling more land, until it became so familiar in the sight of the citizens of Washington, that even the boys would cry out, "There goes the *treasury* keg!" This is the manner in which the patent friends of the poor man occasionally find means to promote his interests!

I recollect travelling one morning through a dense forest, upon a very bad road, in the state of Ohio. I met a wagoner with three horses attached to his wagon — a man on horseback, with a musket or rifle on his shoulder, on each side of the wagon — and the Receiver of public money at the Land Office, inside of the wagon, poising a musket with fixed bayonet. As I was acquainted with the Receiver, he told me, in the course of conversation, that he had a wagon-load of specie, which he intended to deposit in the Clinton Bank of Columbus. A few days after, I saw Clinton Bank notes refused for land at the Land Office! It appeared to me that the whole operation was like trusting with the care of your silver, a man whose note you would refuse to take in payment of a sale of property! At all events, the Specie Circular was rendered, in this way, of little value in checking land speculations. I need say no more to prove how difficult it must be for a poor man to secure lands at twenty-five cents an acre, while they are being rendered so highly valuable to the speculator who can afford to wait a few years, by the rapidly increasing settlements around them, and the projects for internal improvements which the designing politician has power to hasten or delay, as his interest may guide him. The honest administration of the Public Domain for the public good would dictate that the Government should make appropriations for the draining of the swamp lands of the Domain, from time to time, as the natural settlement of the country calls them into requisition for other uses than mere common pasture ground; and the lands should be charged with the expense of this drainage. In this way, the actual settler would acquire them at a much cheaper rate than through the hands of speculators purchasing them at twenty-five cents an acre, with a view to winning large future profits from the farmer.

That such unremitting efforts should be made to sacrifice this vast public interest, can only be explained by the facility which great capitalists and corrupt politicians enjoyed under the system of forestalling, almost gratuitously, the immensely increased value to be given to the lands by projected railroads, and for which the actual settler could not afford to wait. Mr. Polk's administration closed its career in the midst of expenditures as prodigal as those of any that preceded it.

Gen. Z. Taylor, the hero of Buena Vista, succeeded to the Presidency after James K. Polk. In the early days of this Administration, California asked to be admitted as one of the states of the Union. This application produced an excitement upon the subject of slavery, such as the country had never before witnessed. Men in the North and in the South, with unblistered tongues, openly avowed the intention of effecting a disunion of the states! A compromise was effected between the sections by that noble patriot, Henry Clay, that brought about a degree of good understanding satisfactory to all who desire nothing more for their country, for themselves, and for their posterity, than that these

United States should continue to harmonize in union to the latest period of time.

Upon the death of Gen. Taylor, Millard Fillmore succeeded to the Presidency, in July, 1850. This Administration is not marked by any efforts to reform abuses, either in the expenditure of money or the management of the Public Domain. Like its immediate predecessors, it suffered the squandering of the public lands as grants to states, counties, and railroads, to the extent of millions of acres.

Franklin Pierce was inaugurated President of the United States in March, 1853; and, during the first session of Congress, the House of Representatives voted a farm of one hundred and sixty acres, as a free gift to all who can and will accept of it.

The immense riches we possess in the Public Domain, which, if applied for the benefit of all, especially in the way I have indicated, would free us from most of those threatening evils which are fearfully hastening us on the inevitable march of national decay, has induced me to offer the foregoing comparison, to show how carefully and equitably this Domain was guarded for the promotion of vast national objects, up to the time when Gen. Andrew Jackson was elected to the Presidency; and with what pertinacity, since that time, it has been squandered and misapplied for the benefit of the few. To me it appears plain, that if the lands, yet remaining unsold, should be graduated in price *according to their real value*, and sold in proportion to all actual demands for settlement, speculation would cease upon the Public Domain, and, in the end, the industrious farmer, in whose hands alone these lands can be rendered valuable to the country by their productiveness, would obtain them at a cheaper rate than by reaching them through the intermediate agency of speculators, in the " free gift " scheme.

Having already seen that the pre-emption laws really lay at the root of all the disasters of the country in the year 1840, it would be folly, if not madness, after the experience we have had in these pre-emption laws, to attempt the system which looks to free gifts of one hundred and sixty acres, on the false pretence of benefitting the poor man. The true policy of our Government consists in a strict adherence to the fundamental principles of the Constitution, whereby all citizens are acknowledged to possess equal rights in relation to the national property, as well as to political protection. Let us, then, repeal all laws which have a partial bearing; aiming, with singleness of purpose, at the enactment of such only as will secure the greatest interests, and sustain the equal rights of the WHOLE PEOPLE. The result of this general policy cannot fail to be universally beneficial upon every interest. Let the Public Domain become settled by the force of progressive population, as dictated alike by reason, justice, and the voice of nature! A population that doubles itself every twenty-five years, will not be long in bringing our Public Domain under cultivation, without causing any violent reaction upon the interests of the country. But more especially would the peculiar applications I have proposed for the Public Domain enhance this general beneficial result. Under such a course of action, we should soon see large towns growing up in the southern states, from the enlargement of the means of mechanical labour; commerce would no longer have the effect of concentrating the business interests of the country into one or two large capitals; the Atlantic cities of the South would rise to a condition of prosperity approaching to that of those of the North; the interior towns would flourish in all of the states; and, by offering to all the means of happiness, without the necessity of too closely concentrating the population at any one point, they would secure us against the social and political evils which are the necessary growth of all large cities, whilst we should be more generally placed in the most enlarged enjoyment of the good connected with them.

The institution of slavery, when looked at in all its bearings upon ourselves, either within our boundaries, or at a distance beyond them, is of a character that must be fully inquired into before we can understand the magnitude of the evil we are nursing for the destruction of the peace, safety, and happiness of the nation. If, in this inquiry, it has been proved that the prosperity of the nation is endangered by this institution, then the most appropriate national means to remove the evil, ought to be used with the greatest energy, upon the principle of the high natural law of self-preservation. But while the application of this law is made the basis of national action, neither justice nor humanity must be lost sight of; especially when a captive is to be dealt with. The nature of the captivity must be duly considered, and the security of all the safe and practicable immunities of the dependent must be strictly guarded by national honour. If the captive have any rights, whether by race or nation, then we cannot deal with him *personally* in protecting these rights. The honour and dignity of ther nation require that he should be dealt with *nationally*, or generically.

I contend that the brute force by which the African was torn from his native land does not destroy his nationality of character, any more than the capture of an enemy in war would destroy the nationality of the captive. But this brute force gives a peculiarity to African captivity that does not belong to captivity occurring where a formidable resistance is made, and where, if justice is not done to the vanquished, that justice will be demanded as a national right by the commonwealth of nations, agreeably to the doctrines of international law. But now, when nearly all the civilized nations of the earth have united in the determination that this brute force shall no longer prevail against Africa, I contend that the people of the United States are in honour bound to decide what this African captivity is; whether it is a merely personal captivity, or whether abstract justice still secures to the African his national rights, notwithstanding his present inability to maintain them.

If the brute force that brought the race amongst us does not destroy its national rights, then, as the fundamental laws of the Union do not confer upon Congress the power to decide the question of African captivity, I have proposed that it shall take steps to secure a national convention to decide upon the actual condition of the slave, and that this convention, if it should determine to restore the African to his nationality, should at once organize a Board of Trustees for the government of the Public Domain; the moiety of the proceeds of which are at once sufficient and highly appropriate to the task of restoring the American African to his native land. This I propose as absolutely essential to the preservation of the PEACE, THE SAFETY, THE HAPPINESS, THE PROSPERITY, THE MORAL DIGNITY, AND THE HONOUR OF THE NATION.

But, should the Congress of the United States refuse to aid in bringing about the application of the necessary portion of the riches derivable from the Public Domain, to the purpose of securing to the African his nationality, and to this country the fame and glory proper to a consistent, Christian and humane people; should it prefer to confer these riches upon the land speculator; should the people agree to submit to this unprofitable, unholy, and unpatriotic decision, and refuse, in their sovereignty, to take the necessary steps to secure the repeal of such squandering laws as have already passed the House of Representative of the United States at the present session; should they rather choose to shut their eyes upon the encroachments of a corrupt Administration, as they did during the approach and consummation of the declaration of war against Mexico; should they, in sleepy and enervated apathy, look upon the subjugation of their rights with a sluggard indifference; should they, in addition to all this, look upon the brute force which is made to bear upon the African within our borders, and which wrested him from his native land, as being compatible with the dignity and honour of the nation; should they determine to regard his natural rights with as much indifference as they regard their own sovereign and republican rights, in spite of the noble evidence which Liberia has already given of its capacity, when enlightened, for self-government:— then I proceed to examine, not only the probable result of such ignoble action upon the downward progress of our own Government, but also, and more especially, the inevitable future of slavery in the United States, if rendered permanent by our apathy and corruption.

In relation to our own Government, it has been shown that lawlessness is now permitted to riot in defiance of statutes by which the acts of the outlaw are declared to constitute trespass or treason, as the case may be; that the Government has not the power nor the will to punish such offences; that the power to do so is lost by the undue extension of territory, while this extension of territory continues to be sought for by unjustifiable means, as has been shown in the annexation of Texas and the acquisitions secured by the Mexican War—all with a view to the extension of slave territory. The same thing is proved by the attempts, of a most unlawful character, which have been recently made upon the Island of Cuba, and upon Sonora and Lower California, by citizens of the United States — these unworthy traitor citizens undoubtedly pursuing their schemes with a twofold anticipation: first, that, by the annexation of these provinces to the United States, they would increase the area of slave territory, and secondly, that a rich harvest would be reaped from their own previous creation of new state debts, which, like that of Texas, might be afterwards assumed by the United States, to their dishonest profit.

That these trespasses upon the rights of other nations will continue so long as the laws against such transgressions are not strictly enforced, cannot be doubted. It is far more than probable that the Island of Cuba and all Mexico may be brought under the sovereignty of the United States by just such means as were resorted to in Texas, especially if the United States should consent to pay the debts which these traitors to their country, the filibusters, contract, by issuing bonds carrying with them an exorbitant premium. If this policy of the acquisition of territory is not arrested, and the Island of Cuba and Lower California should be annexed with the intention of extending the limits of slave territory, (which would be the inevitable consequence of such acquisition,) then, a strong sentiment in the North opposed to the extension of slavery, which now lies dormant under the restraint of the Constitution, would be aroused to prevent that extension, and we should immediately find the people divided into two great political parties—the slavery and the anti-slavery parties. The Abolitionists have a political organization even now, and if such a state of things should occur, who can doubt that they would gain the ascendant in political power? Then, would not the slave-holder find himself under the necessity of defending his constitutional rights, even if their defence should demand the last argument of kings?

The Constitution of the United States gives Congress no power to control the institution of slavery: it belongs exclusively to the sovereignty of the states. Therefore it is plain, that any political power that the Abolitionists might bring to bear upon the slave states, in violation of the sovereignty of these states, would lead to a dissolution of the Union; and, as the Abolitionists, as a political party, could *enforce* no exactions upon the slave states, without creating a civil war, their zeal for the benefit of the slave or the honour of the country, tends in a wrong direction; for the resistance to the admission of new slave states into the Union, which, under the circumstances just mentioned, the North would feel bound to make, could have no other possible effect than the dissolution of the Union, which might probably be effected by common consent at first.

Such must be the consequences to this Union, however much the patriot may regret the necessity, if the agitations which have already nearly convulsed the nation to dissolution, are aggravated by the early acquisition of Lower California, with other portions of Mexico, or the Island of Cuba. Indeed, it may fairly be asserted, that the question of slavery has already weakened the bonds of union, and without any further acquisition of territory, may lead to a civil war; especially as perfect, full, and immediate emancipation, together with the political enfranchisement of the slave, is demanded by the most inflammatory, fanatical, and anti-constitutional portion of the Abolition party. It must be acknowledged, however reluctantly we admit the fact, that the parties which have controlled our destinies, with a single eye to selfish purposes, to the exclusion of the present and future interests of the country, have driven this question into a position by which the union of the states is most seriously endangered; for we cannot suppose, on the one hand, that the Abolitionists will cease agitating it, or, on the other, that the slave states will bow, in their sovereignty, to the will of the Abolitionist. The only possible mode of settling this question, if slavery is to remain permanent, seems to be the separation of the free states from the slave states.

Yet, even should this agitation lead to a separation of the Union, with all the disgrace attached to so ignoble a deed — whether the result be accomplished by common consent or civil war — still the progress of time will develop the destiny of the North and the South in relation to government, population, and all other things appertaining to a nation. Now, in case this separation is brought about, as slavery connects itself with the South as a theoretical necessity, let us examine what time will do for the South under the more favourable alternative — that of a peaceable separation. As I] have proposed a hundred years for the removal of the African, we will limit this examination of future probabilities to a like period of time. Allowing thirty-three years for the slave population to double itself, 3,500,000 slaves would increase in numbers, in one hundred years, to more than 28,000,000. For the better security of the master it would be requisite that this increased population should be as widely dispersed as possible. Acquisitions of territory would become essentially necessary for this purpose.] As it would be impossible to acquire this territory from the North, it would be sought after in the South. Mexico would be subdued for the extension of slavery, if practicable. If not of easy conquest as a whole, she would be attacked at points where she is powerless for defence, as is now the case in Lower California. Why are our ships of war not now on the coast of Lower California, protecting Sonora against the traitors who have disturbed the peace of a friendly nation? The next step would probably be, the acquisition of the Island of Cuba. The moment this step is taken, the pains and penalties of the South, in consequence of her unyielding grasp of slavery, will begin to be seriously felt; for it will be found that a hatred of the institutions of slavery will not cease to exist in the North. Although no violent manifestations of this hatred may be allowed, yet every legal means will be resorted to in order to keep the slave government in constant fear of consequences. The legal means which the North will adopt to render slavery as irksome as possible to the South will be, the appropriation of all the unsold portion of the Public Domain, in aiding the free coloured man to go to Africa, as well as enabling every fugitive slave to join him in building up civilization on that continent; for, it must be remembered, that, when African progress is once put fully under way by penetrating the interior with railroads, and establishing free states, and when commerce becomes active between Africa and the *Northern* United States, every free coloured man will carry *his memory* with him to the land of his forefathers, and that fatherland will be found to afford the best asylum and the most enlarged freedom for the fugitive slave. Labourers will be in demand there, and capital as well as feeling will be engaged in transporting all fugitives there, and encouraging the slave to abscond, to swell their numbers.

There is no escape from the conclusions I have now arrived at. It must be recollected that the inconsiderate and pertinacious agitators of the slave question, as it affects these United States and especially the slave-holder and slave states, have already " carried the war into Africa," and there will be no peace upon any other principle than such as I propose : — Justice to Africa by a common effort of justice to ourselves!

The moment an effort is made by the Southern states to annex the Island of Cuba, the North will protest. It will be claimed that the Island of Cuba is the principal of a group lying upon the Gulf of Mexico and the Caribbean Sea, belonging to the entire continent of America, and having relations in point of interest common to both North and

South America; that the colonial vassalage in which these islands have long been held by European powers, has exerted an oppressive bearing upon the prosperity, not of the islands only, but the continent also; for, as these powers regulate the commerce of the islands, the exaction of duties and tonnage by them has continually operated to the prejudice of the nations on the continent to which these appendages properly belong by nature; that the time has arrived when neither the Northern United States, Mexico, South America, nor Central America, can ever allow the Southern states to annex the Island of Cuba. It will be given as a reason for this decision, that the mercantile exactions of the Southern states, after annexation, would be equally prejudicial to the interests of all the nations of the American continent. It would be claimed, therefore, on the principle of self-defence and the balance of power, that these islands must be endowed with an independent nationality, under the guarantee of all the continental nations; and the independence of the Island of Cuba from all immediate control by any continental power would be not only of the highest importance, but actually essential to the maintenance of a national government in the West Indies. Besides, it will be urged, that, in consequence of the growing importance of the civilized government in Africa, the independence of these islands has become necessary, to prevent African influence from controlling what really belongs to America. It cannot be doubted for one moment that, if Africa should receive no other aid in the progress of civilization than that which the Colonization Society can give her, and if the negro should still be held in bondage on these islands, three generations will not pass away before the roar of African cannon will resound upon the shores of the Island of Cuba, demanding the restitution of the slave!

When this day shall come, and come it will if the negro continues in bondage, then the great day of trial for the South will also be at hand. With 28,000,000 of a servile race in her fields, in her forests, in her dwellings, listening to the battle shouts of their free brethren re-echoing along her shores, where will she be? Whither will she turn for aid? The pillar of cloud by day, the pillar of fire by night, will bewilder her march and her councils; the waters, long piled up on either hand till an oppressed race has fulfilled its destiny in the land of its servitude, will collapse! Hope pales, and humanity shudders at the scene. Let us draw the curtain.

CHAPTER VII.

A PLAIN TALK WITH THE FREE MAN OF COLOUR IN THE UNITED STATES.

Motives for the African Exodus — The Slave-master generally kind, yet Humanity demands Emancipation — The Establishment of African Nationality essential both to Freeman and Slave — Wrong Views and Practice of the Abolitionists — Political and Social Equality impossible for the Free Coloured Man here — Consequence of attempting it — America has nothing to offer him which he should accept in exchange for African Independence — Political objects of Abolitionists — Unconditional Emancipation would cause Civil War — Condition of the African in Civil War — Possibility of a peaceful Separation of the Union — Condition of the African Race in that case — Two distinct Races cannot dwell together on a footing of Equality — True Political Position of the African in America — He is still a Captive — Rights of Captives — Peculiarities of African Captivity, and their Political Consequences — Reasons why the Coloured Man should favour Colonization and African Nationality, even if Public Aid be denied him — Climate of Africa compared with our own Country — Danger of Delay — British Settlements — Effects of African Progress on Slavery — Consequences of attempting to attain Political Power here — Folly of depending upon National Philanthropy — Is there Labour enough for all ? — Proposed Exploration of Africa by Free Blacks — Its vast possible Consequences — Concluding Appeals.

IN considering the measures proposed for the exodus of the African — measures which aim at the removal of the whole race, both freeman and slave, in the space of one hundred years — the full understanding of the scheme and his own connection with it, will be of the utmost interest to the free coloured man; and his hearty co-operation will be of the highest importance to himself and to Africa. In fact, that co-operation will be essential to the effective execution of the scheme at the commencement, and, therefore, to the ultimate success of the entire plan.

With you, my coloured friends, especially those of you who are freemen, I desire to have a talk upon this all-important subject of your exodus to your fatherland, in order that you may fully understand the reasons which render your departure not only desirable to the nation, but of the highest importance to yourselves, and essential to the future elevation of your race.

The Abolitionist has secured your ear by his efforts in claiming for you rights that he can never establish, and has thus induced you to consider him as your best friend. In this regard for him, you do your own race a direct injury, which falls with especial weight upon your enslaved brother of the South. You cause the point of the nail that closes his shackles to be turned in and clinched into his very flesh. The claims of the Abolitionist impel the master of the slave to struggle perpetually to secure a broader field and longer duration for the enchainment of your race, than he would do, if the continual agitation of the subject did not keep him in a state of perpetual alarm, lest his legal and constitutional rights as a citizen may be wrested from him, by the force of a popular clamour, based upon the plea of humanity, and abstract but impracticable justice.

That most admirable book, Uncle Tom's Cabin, written in open hostility to the Southern institutions, is truthful in representing that sympathy, kindness, and generosity really predominate in the general character of the slave-master; so that feeling and good treatment of the slave constitute the rule, while the horrible abuses and cruelties not less vividly portrayed in the work, are but the exceptions. But these exceptions are of such a character as should induce a generous and humane people to seek, by proper means, the emancipation of your enslaved brethren. And, even of your own condition, it may be remarked with propriety, that the wealth, the education, and the comforts of living which some of you attain to in the North, are exceptions to the general rule of oppression, disability, and suffering, which even as freemen you endure. Your situation here, as freemen or slaves, requires that you should look to your own land for nationality and an open road to honourable advancement. Here it never has been, never will be, never can be offered to you.

Mrs. Bird, a character in Uncle Tom's Cabin, is

represented as receiving a temporary visit at home from her husband, during the session of the Ohio Legislature, he being a senator of that state. She learns that he had voted for a law for the arrest of fugitive slaves in the state of Ohio, and their return to their owners. Taking the humane side of the question, and stating to her husband that he himself would not obey the law, she grows so earnest and eloquent in her appeals, that her husband exclaims,

"Mary! Mary, my dear! Let me reason with you."

"I hate reasoning, John," replies the wife, "especially reasoning on such subjects. There's a way you political folks have of coming round and round a plain, right thing, and you don't believe in it yourselves, when it comes to practice. I know you well enough, John; you don't believe it's right any more than I do; and you wouldn't do it any sooner than I."

In this abolition argument, humanity is made to look no further than to the isolated cases of suffering, and a desire for liberty, upon the part of your race. The whole practical result of the plot of the Cabin is this:—George Harris, Eliza his wife, with Jim and his mother, all fugitive slaves, are carried forward by the aid of Abolitionists, to Upper Sandusky, and there placed on board a steamboat, on their way to Canada and freedom. Now, in the whole course of this abduction, the laws of the land are evaded by a cunning dictated by humanity,— by the appeals of individual suffering, painted in the strongest colours. When George Harris declares he would purchase his liberty, if necessary, at the expense of the lives of his pursuers, or die in the attempt, the humanity of the Abolitionists sympathizes with him most fully; but when the necessity actually occurs, and Loker is shot, their cunning leaves George Harris and Jim to fight their own battles, and take all the responsibility. Now observe, also, that when the fight is over, the same humanity displays itself towards the wounded slave-catcher, in spite of the despicable character of the ruffian. Surely you must yourselves perceive that a humanity, however intense in your favour, that recommends violent resistance on the part of your brethren, the slaves, would soon be transferred to the wounded of the white race, if this resistance should extend itself beyond an isolated case.

In the claims of the Abolitionist, set forth in the elaboration of the story of these fugitives, reason is discarded, and humanity alone is permitted to break down every other consideration. It even causes a grave senator, who, under the influence of reason and patriotism, has just voted for a fugitive slave law as the best means of securing the peace and happiness of the whole nation, to bow in humiliation, in obedience to the claims of humanity, and to violate that law for the happiness of an individual! Can you not perceive that a plan which proposes to elevate your social and political condition as a people, by means that can be applied to individual cases only, must be of little or no service to you as a distinct race, with whom not even the semblance of social equality will ever be permitted here?

You can never raise yourselves into political power, or social standing in this country, except by force; and if force should give you that power (which I presume it never will), *you* would place *us* under a control as servile and exacting as *we* now exercise over *you*.

Do not answer me as Hazael did the Hebrew Prophet of old, — "Is thy servant a dog that he should do this great thing?" Recollect that you have already learned to flourish the whip over your own blood and kin, in the southern states, where some of you have grown rich, and are even now slave owners.

Such are the admonitions of nature, and the experience of the nations that have felt the evils which arise, wherever distinct races of men have been commingled with each other under one nationality. Reason, too, proclaims that no human power, short of the active benevolence of the entire people, can place you in a condition of social equality; and that even this benevolence can only accomplish the result by giving you a distinct nationality, which is impossible on the American continent. *George Harris* tells you this, after the experience that taught him how limited was the power of his friends, the Abolitionists. He tells *them* that, after having considered the subject well, he does not desire to accept even all that they could secure for him in America. He tells them that the scheme of colonization in Liberia promises the only hope of nationality and emancipation for his enslaved and suffering race. Does it not strike you that these abolitionist appeals for your political elevation, by which your sympathies are enlisted, your hopes raised, and your desires inflamed into the belief that you can do much for the cause of freedom by proclaiming your own rights,—does it not strike you, I say, that these appeals look more to the political agitation that may elevate white men to power in the government, than towards anything that they can practically accomplish for your benefit? Surely, if you understood the relations you actually hold towards this country, and remembered the fact, that five out of six of your entire race in America are enslaved, whatever abstract claim to equality may be made for you, you would see, at once, that no political party holding the reins of power, which should attempt your unconditional emancipation and political elevation, could produce any other effect than the dismemberment of the Union, by the worst of all calamities, a civil war!

In such a war, you yourselves, with no power to control events, would remain the passive objects of contention. You would be made the sufferers. In such a convulsive scene of disaster and dismay as the political ascendency of the Abolitionist policy would render inevitable, the only hope for your race would be in the most perfect and complete inaction; for, in a struggle so fearful, which would shatter in fragments the Constitution of the most free Government upon earth, if you should raise a hand in defence of what you are taught to consider your natural and "inalienable rights;" if you should attempt to carry out the doctrine you are now daily taught from the pulpit and the rostrum; that, an opportunity for freedom once presented, the means of resistance, however violent, are admissible; — extermination would be your inevitable fate.

The very humanity widely diffused throughout the United States, which now looks upon you as a sufferer labouring under many privations, and truly commiserates your condition, without any obvious and effective means of relieving you,—would seek, in such an event, for objects of compassion among, and expand itself in sympathy with, our own race, of whose sufferings you would be the authors. Such would inevitably be the effect of any violent action on your part; and this reaction would carry with it your entire destruction. Can you doubt this? If you do, I tell you that a nation which systematically, and at any cost, even that of bloodshed, has removed, in gradual progression, one race of men out of the way of its advancement, and is, even now, penning the remnant of that race within the most limited and constantly narrowing circle; if their passions should ever become excited by any enormities committed by you, would bring to bear upon you the weight of their power, to your prompt and utter annihilation!

Can you not draw a line of distinction between the results of the philanthropy displayed by the Abolitionists in isolated cases of fugitives — which is continually held in your view as proof of their friendship and goodwill towards you — and those which would certainly follow a national demonstration, such as they promise you? Do you not see, that, thus far, by an unprofitable agitation, they have produced nothing more than a proper sympathy for your condition, which they could have brought about by other and more moderate means, if as zealously pursued? Do you not perceive that, by awakening this feeling in a manner unnecessarily violent and irrational, they have tightened the bonds and abridged the privileges of your enslaved brethren? Can you even suppose for a moment, that, if those friends of yours upon whom you so much rely, should ever succeed to the administration of the Government, they would attempt to effect the realization of your hopes? They could not do it. The gulf that would stand wide open in their view, into which that attempt would plunge both them and you, would deter them! The spectres of a civil war and crushed Constitution, would rise to frighten them from any measure of emancipation for the slave, or social or political elevation for yourselves. That national Constitution which, as they pretend, does not stand in the way of extending to your race and all mankind rights equal with our own, would be found to present a barrier over which they could not leap.

It may happen, indeed, though very improbable, that a peaceful division of the Union may take place, if an increase of slave states by acquisition of slave territory, at the cost of the Northern states.

M

should be insisted upon by the South; as I have shown elsewhere. But, in what respect would you be benefited by such a change? At the South, your brethren would still remain slaves, more severely restrained in proportion to the efforts of the Abolitionists to favour their escape. At the North, you would remain as you are; for the North would oppose your political and social elevation as strongly as the South resists the emancipation of your brethren! Two distinct races never did, and never will, exist on an equality under one single government.

However much the harmony of the Government of the United States may be disturbed by the agitation of slavery, that institution cannot be reached, or the emancipation of the slave effected, by the national Government, nor even by the action of any number of sovereign states, aided by that of the Abolitionists of all the states combined, in defiance of the laws of one particular Commonwealth.

In calling your attention, then, to the proposed plan for the emancipation and elevation of your race, which has been the chief subject of the foregoing pages of this book — a plan which, unlike that of the Abolitionists, is both general and practicable—allow me to enter with you into an inquiry as to what your natural and political rights in this country really are.

The first question that naturally presents itself in a national point of view, with relation to your claim of *citizenship* in this country, is this:—Are you still a captive here or are you not? That your ancestors came here as captives, none will deny; and if it cannot be shown that this captivity has ever been annulled — if no national proclamation or declaration of rights has ever been specifically extended to your race — then you are, in the eye of the law, as much a captive *now*, as you were on the first day of your captivity; and your title to equal rights with those who hold you in captivity is no stronger *now*, than it was a hundred years ago; so that, in every correct view of your peculiar captivity, you are still as much an African in nationality, as you were in the first days of the captivity of your race! No such bill of rights has ever been uttered; and therefore the question must be decided in the affirmative.

But, although it may be said that you have no national or lawful claim to citizenship here, yet you have a strong claim upon the humanity and justice of the nation, from the peculiar nature and history of your captivity. The fact that the depravity and defenceless condition of the nations from whom you were originally dragged by force, have rendered them powerless to demand your restitution, viewed in connection with the oppressions to which you have been subjected in America, gives you this indisputable claim. Nor have these unhappy circumstances weakened in any degree your national rights; so that, as long as you are held in confinement, or are only allowed liberty upon parole, the state which, having put you under this restraint, or upon this parole, still refuses to assist any of you who desire to return to your proper nationality in accomplishing this purpose, gives you just cause of complaint. A nation that measures out justice to a captive only when compelled to do so, may still make *necessity* an excuse for not doing *right*, but can neither lay claim to voluntary justice, nor to self-respect.

Humanity prompts kind treatment to the captive; but his release may be prevented by a higher law—that of *self-preservation*. In cases where captives are the subjects of a power capable of demanding their release, on the ground that they owe allegiance to the power making the demand, the release may be made to depend conditionally upon the payment of special damages received, expenses incurred, or any other considerations; but a positive refusal to release the captive on proper terms, cannot be defended on any other ground than self-preservation: but when detained under this plea, neither the nation making the demand, nor the captive himself, has any just cause of complaint, *provided he is treated with humanity.*

There may be cases of captivity in which humanity itself will bar the door, while putting on sackcloth and ashes, and mourning over the necessity that self-preservation imposes on the nation, for the security of its institutions. You will at once perceive how readily the peace and happiness of a nation might be destroyed by the admission of a race of captives to citizenship, rather than restoring them to their proper allegiance; especially if the race should differ very widely from the captors. Dangers may sometimes be found to present themselves from *men of the same race* being admitted into a nation upon terms of perfect equality, on the simple plea of humanity, without any regard to policy. Indeed, upon this principle, a Government may so put aside all prudent guards, that the deepest designs of treason may be perfected under the appearance of perfect acquiescence in the law, until, by a joint or combined effort, the Government may be destroyed for want of vigilance at a moment when it believes itself perfectly secure.

But *your* captivity is of a character peculiar to itself. Your country is too deeply degraded to demand your restitution to your allegiance; the limited liberty you possess renders you powerless in your own defence, or the defence of your slave brethren, and yields you no opportunity to elevate your own nation, so long as you look for political elevation in the nation that oppresses you. To aspire to political position in a country in which the condition of negro slavery is rendered irremediable by the general Government, under one of the fundamental provisions of the Constitution itself, is sheer folly: and this fact alone *should be* a sufficient reason to induce you to seek a nationality in your own land. In judging of the propriety of so doing, there are several considerations by which you ought to be governed. The nature and cause of your oppression should be your first inquiry. If you cannot find any other plea for your captivity than the avarice of a nation, grasping at wealth and power through your labours and energies, your judgment ought, at once, to dictate a yielding to necessity, under a full conviction that, so long as you allow yourselves, or can be made, to minister to this avarice, your oppression and that of your enslaved brethren will continue. You must recollect that you were stolen from your country; and, for the reason that that country could not punish the thief, you were openly acknowledged to be stolen property, in the shape and form of human beings! Yes! men who were the subjects of nations claiming for their rule of moral conduct the teachings of Christianity. Merchants governed by the laws of Christian nations, have traded in your flesh from first to last, with no other consideration for *you* than the pieces of silver you would sell for! And your value was found in the capacity you have for labour!

You are valued as much for the power you have to labour *now*, as you were *then*; so that, to secure the full benefit of your labours, you have been, you are, and you ever will be, denied all political and social elevation or social equality in this country. What plea can overthrow this argument in favour of compelling your services, while unscrupulous worshippers of mammon are, with few exceptions, the leading politicians who seek to administer the Government for selfish ends? In the pursuit of political power by statesmen of this stamp, all good example is ridiculed; the future remains a sealed book, and the present is regarded only for the spoils of office.

If the cries and anguish of your kindred when torn from their homes; if the horrors of the slave ship; if the crushed and broken heart of the victim of rapacity; if his shoulders, bruised and lacerated under the lash of the task-master; if pity and commiseration for your hapless and forlorn oppression — if *all these things* have not sufficed to arrest your captivity even to this hour, where is your future hope? If a powerful nation — a nation that ought to be as magnanimous as it is great — has failed to inquire into the means that should relieve the oppressed; if it has failed to offer to a degraded nation a compensation for the wrongs that have been heaped upon her; even refusing to follow the example of the leading European powers, by acknowledging the American colonies in Africa, founded by humanity, supported by private means, and cherished and sustained by your patriotic American brethren — if you see around you *all these things,* let me conjure you, my coloured friends, to examine well your true relations to the sordid spirit of power which refuses to render you justice! Deceive yourselves no longer with the hope that the little dribbling rill of Abolition will one day empty the ocean of your wrongs! When you have learned your true position in this land, then let Reason point you to your duty. If she should teach you that the grapes growing upon the vines of "humanity and equal rights," which are assiduously cultivated for your use by the Abolitionists, do not grow too high for you to reach them, and that they will not be sour when grasped, surely your nativity, and the graves of your kindred and friends will plead in natural and strong language that you should stay here and eat them. But if Reason should tell you that the storms of agitation by which these vines are nourished, will probably prevent the fruit from ripening, and thus wreck all your hopes at last, you will have less sagacity than the fox in the fable, if you do not pronounce these grapes *sour!* Again; if Reason should point out your duty to Africa, by showing that such grapes, even if won, would be but a small compensation for the horrors and consternation of the African slave-hunt; for the suffocation and agonizing death of your brethren in the slave ships; for the bones of your race left bleaching on the bottom of the ocean in every channel, from Africa to Christian lands; for the spirit bruised, the heart broken through sufferings such as these, and expatriation into unmitigated slavery; for the separation of man and wife, mother and child — if Reason and Religion should unite their voices to remind you that, even here, during your sojourn in the wilderness of woes and the dungeons of despair, you have been entrusted with the keys that shall unlock the doors, and open the windows of the houses of your fathers, that the winds of Heaven may sweep away the foul air of superstition and the very memory of oppression; that you are the appointed missionaries to carry there American freedom, and light up the chambers with the burning and never-fading lights of Christianity; that, to fit you for this task, you have been permitted to endure these accumulated miseries, and that, in fulfilling it, you will reap full compensation for them all — surely you will no longer "lust after the flesh-pots of Egypt," but will steadfastly pursue the line of duty dictated by both natural and Divine revelation! You will surely regard as futile, the claims of "humanity and equal rights," as made applicable to your case by the Abolitionists in this country, and will join with me in entreating for *a wider humanity*, acting upon a broad national scale, and calculated to promote your exodus; believing, with me, that any form of humanity that does not embrace your fatherland within its mantle, can only excite a useless pity for your oppressed condition — barren of all grand and permanent result!

But now you may begin to fear that the national humanity I claim for you will not be granted; that Congress will not aid in the initiatory steps of the scheme I propose; and that the people will never think it worth while to move in the matter, because they no longer seem to have the same notions about public affairs, their own rights, the future interests, moral dignity and the glory of the country, that were entertained before the Revolutionary War, and even *after that period,* up to the time of the election of Gen. Jackson. Well, I cannot say that your fears are without reason, when we see men hurrying out of one speculation into another; the deliberations of Congress seemingly having no other end than to multiply private operations in filibuster-born state stocks, private gifts of land for railroads, and free gifts of farms to everybody in the world that chooses to take them!

But you will say, " Perhaps our prospects here are not so bad as you think. We recollect that, a few years ago, the Abolitionists got some men to join them whom they called 'Freesoilers;' and we think it was at Buffalo that they got up a thing they called a Platform; and directly we were told that we were to have free democracy, freedom of speech, and free soil; and the houseless poor would be made rich; and all this was done, we were told, for our benefit more than that of the white man. Yet we must confess we are no better off than we were before, notwithstanding Mr. Van Buren took the lead in our behalf. And when you tell us that the recommendation of Mr. Van Buren to graduate the price of the public lands, and sell that which had been lying in the market for fifteen years *dog cheap,* was only intended to lay the foundation of a great speculation in the land lying six and seven miles, and so on, from the canals, we suppose you mean to say that the knowing ones would have bought it for twenty-five cents an acre, and sold it to the poor settler for five and ten dollars per acre!"

Yes; that is what I mean to say.

" Well then," you will reply, " since *we* are not to have any free gifts of land, we begin to think our masters intend to keep the land, and us too, for the grandest speculation ever yet based upon our rights and the rights of the white poor man!"

With your doubts and your fears, and your questions about political agitations that never have done, and never will do, any good, you prevent me from stating to you that, if Congress and the people should alike refuse to carry out the scheme I propose for your exodus, it is nevertheless your duty to make all the exertions in your power to go to Africa!

The colonization of Africa has taken root in Liberia, Sierra Leone, and the Maryland Colony, where political freedom such as you desire here in vain, is really to be found; a freedom that, *if you will, you can* direct for the good of your whole people; so that your destiny, and that of your country, does not positively depend upon the scheme I have proposed for your assistance. I urge this duty upon you, and upon our own Government alike, for our elevation in national morality, and for your rapid advance in civilization. You may rely upon it that Liberty and Christianity *will* advance in Africa, as certainly as out of the acorn grows the oak, and the sooner you go to nourish this tree of liberty, the better for yourselves and country. Your population in the United States and Canada exceeds 500,000. Let us suppose that a like number should transfer themselves and their interests to their fatherland. We should then behold the organization of five or six states, all raising the flag of African liberty, upon a *black ground* with *white stripes*, with as many stars as states. We should see an active commerce existing between the United States and your country. Only think of this for a moment! African ships moored at the Philadelphia wharves, owned by black captains and merchants; the crews, black sailors; loaded with the riches of Africa, brought to the coast by railroads from the interior and mountain regions—from a rich soil and a salubrious climate! Why; you would all of you be on the wharves, inquiring whether the steamboat which left but six weeks before, had arrived in Africa with your friends on board before they left. You would have confirmation of all the good reports of African progress in freedom and civilization. Of course you would all desire to go to Africa, and all of you who could, would immediately make ready and go. Then, if slavery should still exist in the Southern states, while your ships and steamboats, as well as ours, would be departing from New York and Philadelphia, and arriving from Africa almost daily, you would find that your Abolition friends, (who aid the fugitive to escape from his master, "because it is right to do so," and because "all men are born free and equal," and reason has nothing to do with "the higher laws which give liberty to all,") would conduct the fugitives on board the African ships. They would all be Colonizationists then. Canadian liberty would be too exacting, and of course no longer appreciated by the runaway himself.

But I hear you say, "These things are not so now." That is true; but it is your own fault that this commerce does not already exist in its incipient stages. If you that are intelligent and industrious, and saving of your earnings, had encouraged industry and economy among your people, and if all of you had determined, with a proper patriotism, to carry your wealth and your knowledge of American progress and American liberty to Africa, instead of looking only for the little aid that the Colonization Society can afford you, or suffering yourselves to be beguiled by hopes that can never be realized, (or, if they could be, would still fall short of that happy independence you can secure in Africa,) then you would not have to say, "These things are not so now."

But let it be once understood that your faces are turned *homewards*, and you would find the American merchant ready immediately to furnish all the means necessary for your emigration and commerce; and, in one year, by such a course of conduct, you would see preparations being made to secure the African trade for the mutual benefit of your country and ours.

But you are told that the climate of Africa is sickly, and that men cannot live there. Yet you know that men do live there! This idea is founded upon an inordinate zeal for your equality of rights here, without hope or reason. Surely there can be no difficulty in your understanding the flummery of this argument, after having resided in this country for two hundred years, well knowing all the sufferings and privations of your ancestors, and all the difficulties you yourselves are daily obliged to overcome or yield to.

Liberia should present itself to your mind as a land of promise, to which you can return in the gladness of your hearts; where you could enjoy unmolested liberty with a hope of a happy and free posterity. Should you then be startled by the fact that death levies a heavier tax upon all early settlers of young colonies, than he imposes on well-regulated and long-established communities; should this, I say, be permitted to cool your patriotism and your desire for independence? If so, you will give force to the chief excuse made for your oppression; namely, that you are idle, unambitious, and deficient in the intellectual capacity required to establish self-government or a national character! I believe many of you to be idle and prodigal; but for this, no people have a more reasonable excuse. The first lesson taught you in the process of being lifted from heathen degradation, through a bruised spirit and a broken heart, has caused you to lean with entire dependence upon your master. This has rendered too many of you idle and profligate; and even in your freest condition, the want of proper motives to ambition and exertion has subdued or depressed the power of your intellect. Yet there are many of you who are wealthy and highly intelligent, dignified in manners, moral in sentiment, and capable of appreciating, perhaps with a fervour peculiar to yourselves, the saving health of Christianity. Under such influences, a true patriotism will set you right upon this question of the health of Africa. This question you will answer best by comparing it with the health of other places. Nor could you possibly have been placed upon any portion of the globe where you could so well form a proper estimate of the difficulties which new colonies have to overcome as in this country. Our early history teaches you the difficulties which Virginia, Massachusetts, and all the colonies had to contend with in the beginning. In all of them, disease and death broke down the patriot who sought freedom from an oppression far more supportable than yours; and, by observation, you fully understand our progress. The colonies of Virginia and Massachusetts suffered in the ravages of disease, and the resistance to settlement by the natives, much more than has Liberia; nor was the early advance of any of the colonies of America at all comparable with the progress of Liberia, except in the instance of Pennsylvania alone; this colony being commenced sixty years after that of Virginia. Thus it will be seen that it required sixty years to colonize the coast between Virginia and New York. Even in Pennsylvania, the most favoured of all the colonies, Indian murders upon the frontiers were perpetrated within a hundred miles of Philadelphia. sixty years after the first settlement by William Penn. In 1755, full seventy-seven years after the landing of Penn, and while the whole country west of the Susquehanna river was yet a wilderness, Gen. Braddock was defeated by the Indians! Behold the activity, life, wealth, and prosperity of this colony now!

The progress of Liberia during the first thirty years of its existence, has been far greater than that of this most favoured of American colonies; nor can there be a doubt, that if you will give Liberia the consideration which she demands for the promotion of your own best interests and those of your fatherland, that, in seventy years after its first settlement, or forty-five years from the present time, you will have railroads extending hundreds of miles into the interior, and penetrating well-organized states, inhabited by an industrious, free, and happy people; while, at the corresponding period in the history of Pennsylvania, no other than a horse-path led from one settlement to another in the interior, fifty miles from the capital! Difficulties attended every step of the progress of these colonies, such as will not be met with in Africa; and in addition to all the advantages you will find to aid you in your rapid advancement there, you will have far greater encouragement from this country than England ever afforded to our ancestors. But, if the scheme I have proposed for the work of colonization should be adopted, this plan would not only display, in the loftiest manner, the moral grandeur and dignity of the nation, but it would advance you in civilization with such a startling rapidity, that the settlement of Liberia would commence a new era in the history of nations. No nation upon earth, however powerful, would then be permitted to plant a colony upon the soil of Africa on the principle of colonial vassalage to herself. Nothing short of a free state would be allowed, after you had established even four free states upon the American model.

The British have sent expeditions up the important African rivers in search of cotton fields. They have found a salubrious climate and fertile lands; and it is said that they are making preparations to navigate those rivers, and found establishments; especially on the Chadda, a tributary of the Niger. This fact alone may operate against your perfect political freedom in your own fatherland, unless you act with promptitude, and are backed by the United States in some great national scheme. This seems necessary to save you another great revolution, like to ours, at some future day. No doubt you, too, would even then be enabled to glory in your own "Fourth of July," and in your own "Twenty-second of February:" yet revolutions cost blood; and if you delay your duties, that blood will be chargeable to you. But in the low state of public morals in this boasted country of ours, you must arouse yourselves, and, by your own efforts, secure your own nationality. To persuade you to depend upon the aid I ask for you, would be doing you injustice; especially when 500,000 of you are in a condition not to be restrained from going to Africa as fast as you can make the necessary preparation. Recollect, for your encourgement, that the children of Israel were but 400,000 in numbers, when their exodus from Egypt to the promised land commenced, and that they yet remained in the wilderness for forty years, before even their great standard-bearer was permitted to look in upon it from Mount Pisgah, and *even he* had not the privilege of entering it! But in all this time, and in all the days of Egyptian bondage, these exiles were perfecting themselves, through wrongs and sufferings, for the performance of the vast national duties to which they were appointed. Will you then remain behind in your similar duty? Will you draw no lesson from your parallel history? Will you shut your eyes to its prophetic teaching? With your views turned to Africa, you will feel yourselves ennobled; you will feel that, although you may have no hopes of ever even seeing the "land of promise" yourselves, you have a nation to contend for; you have a Divine mission to fulfil.

The limited freedom Canada can give you, and the equal rights you now contend for here, will appear small gifts in your sight when patriotism shall point to an open field for useful labour in Africa. Then will you become more industrious, more frugal, more intelligent and enlightened: you will study our own history more closely, and your observation of all you can see in our progress will be made applicable to the progress of your fatherland. When your little boy returns from school, you will lay your hand upon his head; you will see in him a future member of Congress, a judge of a court, a Governor of a state in Africa! Such hopes, not merely ideal, will make you better men here; and the reaction of that improvement will make you more respected, even before you leave us. You will see in the future a great blessing in store for your children. You will see that, for the benefit of Africa, no drunkard, idler, or convict ought to be permitted to go there. This last consideration will lead to a more proper care of your children, who are now neglected by too many of you, because you see that a high elevation of character often renders them unhappy here, and unfits them for their humble duties. But when you discover that talents cannot be too highly cultivated for Africa, then indeed will you have motives to actuate your conduct, to which you have as yet been strangers.

I have stated to you that, when you shall determine upon Africa for your home, no longer gazing at the basket of sour grapes, the merchants will keep pace with all your requirements in your transit. And here I want you to bear in mind the certainty that African progress will be vastly more rapid than was that of the American colonies. In consequence of the improved means of transit now at your command, the average time of a passage to Liberia, by means of a good steamboat, will not be more than twenty days, and our sailing ships will perform it in a much shorter time than was required in olden days to perform the voyage from England to America.

You cannot all be off at once, though probably nearly all of you will soon have a desire to go; and, as the Colonization Society, perhaps fortunately, cannot furnish aid to all, the means of the wealthy and intelligent will naturally enable and induce them to lead the way in the elevation of their country from heathen degradation to civilization. This is as it should be; and, the way once clearly open, the demand for labour in the progress of improvement and agriculture will smooth the path for the less fortunate. When you figure to yourselves one state after another, adding their stars to the national stripes, united after the example of the United States, what power can restrain you, my wealthy and intelligent coloured friends, from going to Africa, and commencing your noble mission? Oh, how oppressive and galling will the chains you now wear appear to the awakened aspirant for perfect liberty! But how distant will be the accomplishment of so much good, if you who are capable of regenerating your fatherland, suffer the glory of Africa to rise only through the scanty means of the Colonization Society — means which, in too many instances, it is obliged to bestow upon the recently emancipated slave, whose knowledge of American freedom and civilization is, by necessity, so far below that which you possess!

Can you be idle in so great a salvation for your people? Dare you, in conscience, continue to struggle for a freedom *here*, which, if attained by all your race, would be so far below the independence which Africa holds out to you, whilst the poor and lowly patriot of your tribe is reaping the honour and the glory of building up a nationality for you, which properly belongs to yourselves?

How slow was American colonization for two hundred years; say from 1608 to 1808, when American liberty first asserted the right to protect the oppressed of Europe in all cases where American citizenship was claimed! How rapid has been the flow of immigration, seeking protection under this flag, since that time. The honour, fame, and world-acknowledged glory won by the British convict, and the poor woman sold to the man who refused to abandon the colony of Virginia under the severest trials, are only eclipsed by the high esteem and veneration in which we hold the stern bearing for conscience' sake of the noble patriots who landed upon Plymouth rock! Then, with the assurance that, compared with the early colonists of America, you will have little to suffer, and that *your fame, honour, and glory* will be no less than theirs—because *you too* seek your own freedom and the salvation of your native land—every other consideration ought to be made subservient to a stern duty to your country. Examine into this duty closely; and if you find, as I think you will, that it points to your best interests in Africa, and that you can secure freedom for your enslaved race, better, and in a shorter time, by transferring your means and energy to that continent, than you can by any power you possess or can acquire here, you will of course pursue the line of conduct which it dictates.

But you have other than mere individual duties to perform; others than those which appertain to the redemption of Africa: the securing of your own citizenship there, preparing the way for the poor man, and the redemption of your race. You must not lose sight of your brother still held in slavery here! You ought fully to understand that the sooner you make yourselves strong as a nation, the sooner will the desire for extensive or complete emancipation here be brought about. Whenever Africa becomes strong enough to revive her dormant claim to the fealty of her captive compatriots, she will demand their freedom; and the law of nations will bear out the demand.

It will then endanger the slave-holder in the United States, as much as in the West India Islands, to refuse to emancipate your brethren. I have given it as my opinion, that, if slavery remains unchecked in the United States, the time will come, and that *soon*, when, measured by the clock that records the cycles of nations — say in one hundred years — when more than 20,000,000 of your race will be found, chiefly in the Southern states and in Mexico. I also suppose that, at the end of this short period, the employment of the only means in your power, (that is, the power you 500,000 freemen in the United States possess to control the destinies of your fatherland,) will cause the roar of African cannon to resound upon the shores of the Island of Cuba, demanding the restitution of the slave to his original fealty; and that, then, the great day of trial for the South will have arrived. But, before we get through with this talk, (and I am right glad to have a little talk with you,) I will show you that, if you are slothful, unpatriotic, and apathetic to the interests of your country, your fatherland will present another picture. Before I ask you, however, to look upon the dark side of this picture, I must still suppose that you are particularly interested by the bright side of the prospect exhibited by African freedom, and the elevation of your race; for I cannot flatter myself that all of you who are wealthy and intelligent, and have, or soon might have, the confidence of your people, are *here and now* engaged in encouraging them to foster an African nationality, by inducing them to give up all idea of entering into the affairs of our Government, upon equal terms with us. I must endeavour still more closely to show how utterly impossible it would be for you, or for those you are endeavouring to enlighten, to secure this equality in anything beyond the mere power of voting. I need only point to the vast number of foreigners amongst us, who are courted for their votes. Yet, whenever one of these foreigners has the audacity to ask for office, how his professed friends vote directly against him! When I see that the very considerable amount of wealth and intelligence which you possess is held back from giving Africa that aid of which she stands in so much need, while you publicly contend for equal rights *here*, upon the plea of *nativity*, and are using every effort to have your allegiance transferred from your own country to this, I cannot readily perceive by what infatuation you are guided. If you had observed, as you might and should have done, the dominant character of the Anglo-Saxon, you would have seen how impossible it is that any effort you can make to secure for yourselves an equality of political rights, should prove of any avail.

History teaches that, however great the power of a nation may be, it may decline, grow powerless in its own defence, and pass away — that a hardy and oppressed people may become the rulers of their enervated masters. Your race in this country is four millions strong; and, in a little while, you will number many millions more. While your exertions as labourers enervate your masters, and render them perfectly dependent upon you, they are divided upon all public matters, even to the preservation of the Union! You argue hence that, as you will be all the while growing stronger, one common object may yet unite you in sentiment; so that emancipation and enfranchisement may one day secure office to you, as soon as you can gain majorities in townships or counties. I tell you, that if you reason in this way, you stand on the brink of a precipice! If you had the power, in a single Congressional district, to elect a man of your colour to Congress, and were to enforce your power, it would have the effect of dissolving the Union; therefore, the very idea that you could, by a vote, bring mischief to bear upon us, must forever operate as a bar to your enfranchisement. It is asking too much of a people to put their Government in jeopardy. If such are your motives for contending for the high privilege of voting, I must tell you, in plain dealing, that your hopes will never be realized. Do you not at this moment really believe that, if you had a vote, and were to present one of your own colour for office, in preference to a white Abolitionist, your best friends would turn against you, and that, rather than you should be elected, they would vote for a slave-holder? I do! I will tell you why I do! I have seen men who court the foreign vote, yet who, when a foreigner is presented for office, vote rather for a political native American than permit the election of *their kind, confiding friends!* You may rest assured that if, by any combination of the foreign vote in this country, twenty purely democratic candidates for Congress should be defeated in any one year, even if it were possible that this event should cause no wide-spread sensation throughout the country, it would at least add twenty to the American party. But *it would cause such a sensation!* It would have the effect at once of changing the naturalization laws!

Democracy wants voters; it does not want men that want office, nor inquirers into its policy, beyond what seemingly relates to broad principles and the general good of the country. A closer scrutiny into *the public spoils* is often rewarded by an ejectment from the party. Free democracy also wants voters, upon the same principle no doubt; and to secure your vote, it has raved and still raves about free soil. But you see that the slave democracy has fairly taken the start of the free democracy, and is about giving this free soil to *its own voters;* so that, really, if you had a vote, you would have to give it for nothing. For this slave democracy has all the public lands, the revenues of the country, and the direction of nearly all the state improvements in railroads and canals under its own control; and this whole power is brought to bear in the way best calculated to secure *office* and *private speculation*. This slave democracy will annex a state, and enact the assumption, by the nation, of a state debt, to enrich the politician. It will make a war that shall cost millions of dollars, for no better apparent purpose. Ten or twenty millions of dollars in payment of treaty stipulations are nothing, provided there are private claims enough to warrant the transaction and absorb the money. All these things modern democracy does, without consulting the people at all; the discussion by the people of the subjects that engross its attention, or their advice upon such questions, is not asked for or desired—the thing is done, and there is an end of all argument about it.

Modern democracy is so jealous of its controlling power, that, in all measures of national import which do not affect the pocket of the politician personally, —such as a bank or a tariff—if these measures should happen to favour a conservative policy in the most remote degree, or if the Whig party should claim the credit of originating them, the axe is laid to their root at once, however necessary to the public welfare they may be, although the suspension of specie payments, and the breaking down of the manufacturing interests of the country should stare us in the face.

Doubtless you know more of the liberality of your Abolition friends than I do, (yet I do know some that will put their hands into their pockets to free an individual or a family of slaves,) and you can judge best whether, if they had the power to serve you as a race, they would raise you upon a political equality with themselves or not.

"Why do you talk to us about the evil practices of your public men, and the want of public morals?" asks some wealthy man of colour. "Surely we do not want to interfere any further than this: — as tax-payers and born free, we conceive that we have a right to a vote. Taxation and representation should go together, and we only ask a vote; but we know our places, and we would not interfere with politics, except *to vote.*"

Thus you would *carry the hod* upon election days, as your poorer brethren now do in building our houses. The mere privilege of voting is not worth contending for, without the power of voting for whom you please; and it must be obvious to you that, being men, and disposed even now to grasp at the power by which the destiny of the country is controlled for good or evil, the very moment you could control it for your own benefit, you would do so, to the exclusion of all others! And I sincerely believe that any attempt to obtain a controlling power by means of any combined effort of yours, even in a township or city ward, would bring down the most serious harm upon yourselves. To convince you of this, and in order to prove to you how little your claims will be regarded, I have endeavoured to show you how concentratedly selfish the politician of the present day is; and that he looks only to the promotion of his own ends. In my plan for the elevation of your race, by facilitating your return to your own country, I ask from him the means by which he hopes to purchase voters at the public expense. You cannot be surprised, then, to hear me acknowledge my belief that the motives by which the modern politician is actuated will lead him to refuse to grant, at the present time, the request I make in your behalf. I think, also, that some time will be required for *the people,* in their present state of apathy with regard to the public lands, to find out how much this trust is abused by Congress. It will be some time, before they can be induced to inquire into, and exert their power in removing the Public Domain from the custody of politicians, and giving a proper direction to its management.* I am anxious, too, that you

---

* The scheme of the Pacific Railroad is likely to favour the plans in relation to the Public Domain which are adverted to in this work, because the people will find that the public lands offer the only legitimate means for the construction of this road; and, in order to insure the completion of this great national work, and due economy in the vast expenditures demanded by it in a wilderness far removed from regular settlements, it will be necessary that a proper supervision should be exercised in relation to it. Congress cannot secure economy, even in the ordinary affairs of the Government; and the proposed Board of the Public Domain will doubtless be regarded as a far safer agent for the work.

should take the securing of your freedom and citizenship into your own hands, and in the right way. This is the only excuse I have for speaking to you of our headlong course, so that you should not be too much disappointed if you should receive no such aid as I have demanded for you. Besides; I want to convince you that, if the people would rather see the riches of the country squandered in corrupt or injurious speculation, than that they should aid you, as captives, in restoring you to your natural allegiance, small indeed must be the chance of your securing rights and privileges *here*, in the midst of those who deny you even that justice by which they would be able really to enrich and elevate themselves, if selfishness had not so blinded them to their own interests that they cannot perceive the most obvious truths!

Have you not been repeatedly told by the *Pharaohs* who are not willing to let you go to your fatherland, that this country is large enough to hold all of *you and us*; that there are millions of acres of land to clear up, and houses to build, and all you can desire for happiness here; that it is morally right that you should have all the privileges you contend for; that Africa is no longer your land? And have you not found, when thus reconciled to your hopeless situation, that the hardest work in clearing the farm and building the house was allotted to your share? Has it never occurred to you that the vast amount of labour you perform here, if properly directed and aided by the wealth you possess, would make Africa flourish as a civilized nation? Nor is this all. Has it never occurred to you that you are only tolerated or appreciated here for the labour you can perform? Do you not hear daily, that Europe, at a public charge, empties her jails and poor houses of her paupers and convicts, and sends them to this country to rid herself of a useless portion of her population? Is this right? Certainly not! Yet the nation that does this, claims to take the lead in emancipating the African slave! Can you trust such sympathy? And your Abolition friends claim for you privileges equal with those of the whites, *because it is right!*

Do not trust to the simple declaration of *right*, with a hope that it will be gratuitously enforced, when you see our mother country expatriating the pauper, and using our jails for her convicts! Like the parent, you will find the child. Can you not perceive that, in an overdense population, *you* would be the first to be shipped to Africa, poor and naked, if Africa would receive you?

I tell you candidly, that if you expect national generosity where justice is withheld, you will be disappointed. You can estimate private generosity, and no doubt know how to appreciate it. I know you have had some lamentable experience, especially in some of our cities. This ought to enable you to decide at once against the argument that we have labour enough, and a world large enough, for ourselves and you. Are you not now made to suffer for want of employment, where you come in contact with a white man (it may be the newly-arrived immigrant) for a day's work? Have you not been scattered from your most thickly inhabited quarters in a city, to a distance beyond the suburbs, when you presumed to do the work that the white man claimed as his right? Do you think that any railroad contractor, in any free state in the Union, would dare to employ one thousand of you to do the work upon a railroad? Would any one hundred of you be enabled to unite to build the houses for which you are allowed to carry the brick in the hod, in any of our free cities? Remember the hall that was built for the purpose of bringing you upon a social equality with us, and enabling you publicly to discuss your political rights. Has it not been burned to the ground? You answer "Yes" to all this. But is it right?

I tell you that you have wrongs heaped upon your heads daily. And daily the same question is reiterated, "Is it right?" without bringing you any relief, or advancing you one step in what you claim as right.

If I were not afraid of making my book too large, I would tell you all I know about how shabbily you are treated in regard to all your personal rights, even by the Abolitionist. But, as your country is a vast country, and as it is now in your power, with the knowledge you have gained by absorption in your journey through the wilderness, to become a mighty nation on the earth, it is no more than right that I have made a statement of facts relating to you and us, in order to convince you that all who persuade you not to go to Africa are wrong, and that going to Africa is going to freedom.

I recollect that the Hon. T. H. Benton, in one of his speeches upon the Pacific Railroad, said that, somewhere up the Rocky Mountains, a guide-board would be placed, pointing west, but declaring that such was the shortest way to the east. This caused surprise in all who did not understand that the globe is round. The only difficulty between the Abolitionist and myself is, that he seems to think the earth a plain, as it was supposed to be in ancient times, when men spoke of the "four corners of the earth." In looking over the surface of this plain, the Abolitionist does not see into Africa at all! He merely tells you that he catches a glimpse of the coast of the promontory of that continent, which juts out towards America, and that it is terrible there to behold the ravages of death; that the soil of much of the coast is sterile; that the few of your own people there are tyrants; and that your native brethren are poor and naked. Because of all these things, he tells you that you ought not to go to Liberia. But when I say to you that I conceive it to be one of the highest duties you owe yourselves to go and comfort your poor distressed brethren, many, if not all of you, will think with me. I know many of you who have a strong faith in that book which teaches this duty. You look upon the promises of that book with a faith as full as that which cheered a majority of the children of Israel in their journey through the wilderness — the faith which taught them that their deliverance would be accomplished in the proper time, by the Almighty God, who knows all things best. I know many of you who are full in faith, and, without murmuring, are patiently awaiting the time of *your deliverance* in a trustful hope. I can readily conceive how gladly all of you who are thus confiding would gird your loins for the journey to Africa, if the means I propose for your relief should be granted. How glorious will Africa then appear to your view! How short will seem the hundred years I propose for your gradual return to the home of your fathers, when a definite period is fixed for the freedom of the last captive of your race, instead of the darkness and hopeless uncertainty which obscure that period now! The want of fertility of soil on the *coast* of Africa will no longer be objectionable. You will soon learn that this is no argument against the fertility of the interior, any more than the want of high fertility on the Atlantic coast of this continent is an argument against the fertility of the rich interior. Nor does the sickness of the sea-shore of Africa furnish any better argument in proof of the unhealthiness of climate in the interior, than the sickness at Charleston and New Orleans would furnish against the health of the mountain regions and upland valleys of this noble country. All such arguments will appear false in the nature of things, and will no longer stand in the way of your interests and your duties. Fortunately for you, the elevation of character to which you have attained whilst here (far, far above that which your native brethren possess), places your natural, just, and absolute rights in your own keeping, the moment you arrive upon the soil of your ancestry. As you cannot all go at one time, thousands of you, it is true, can never hope to see the Africa of your choice; but even such will not be the less elevated by the noble purpose and lofty duty which you undertake, or less useful here, in furthering their accomplishment.

Let it be once understood that you desire, for your race, citizenship in Africa, and nowhere else, and those who, from age or other reasons, have no desire to leave America, will find aid and encouragement, *here,* in the education of your children, and in fitting them for Africa. And, as your native country becomes opened more and more widely from year to year, your exodus, and the commerce between your nation and ours will as steadily increase; and just in the proportion of the growth of your nation in commercial importance, and, consequently, in wealth and power, will be the justice rendered to your race in this country. National justice is rather equivocal where there is no power to resist oppression.

To secure, as soon as possible, a point of greatness that will enable you to enter into commercial treaties with the great nations of the earth (which would put you in a position to demand the restitution of your brethren), it appears to me highly desirable, as a first step, that the wealthy amongst you should unite in sending ten or twenty of your most intelligent and enterprising men to explore the regions of the Upper Niger, to win the good will of the natives there, and, by all possible and fair means, to secure the territory necessary for the organization of a future interior state. Let them make a full exploration of the country in relation to roads, mountains and rivers, and report all matters of interest in connection therewith. Such a step once taken, a universal interest in the success of the project would immediately spring up. A free state once organized upon the head waters of the River Niger, African civilization and African power would be secured beyond a doubt; new pursuits would be created, and the sources of labour would be continually enlarged; thus, opening the country for a more rapidly-increasing immigration in each succeeding year. Nor is this all. The immigration of each year would be more and more enlightened. Your wants in Africa would require men of intelligence and knowledge in all the departments of the arts and sciences. Here, they would be educated by your own exertions; for it would be found that such as would remain here, either from choice or necessity, would, each in his proper sphere of duty, be efficient in many ways in forwarding the interests of his country, especially in the proper culture of the talents of his children; and in this matter you would be encouraged by your real friends, to an extent vastly beyond all present calculations. Nor is even this all! This high and patriotic object, and your exertions in promoting it, would make you virtually African citizens at once. It would make you better men and better citizens than any citizenship you could acquire here. It would eventually place your nation in a position to *demand* that the African slave shall be emancipated.

You now, I hope, fully understand that you possess a mighty power *within yourselves*, for the redemption of your fatherland from degradation; for the release of your enslaved brethren upon the West India Islands and in the United States, by and through African nationality; and for securing your own elevation, freedom, and citizenship. Patriotism dictates that you should make every exertion in your power to secure the national blessings Africa has in store for you.

You understand fully, too, what I propose in the form of national aid for your elevation as a people. Nor have I any doubt that, if the pervading sentiment of our whole people could be made to bear upon the subject of your nationality, then, rather than that our ample lands should continue to be squandered so injudiciously, if not iniquitously, as they now are, they would be applied to the purposes I have pointed out, and that full justice would be meeted out to you at last. And now, in naming one hundred years as necessary for the complete accomplishment of your exodus, notwithstanding the vast resources which we might apply to the purpose if we saw fit, I have been guided rather by your interests than by our necessities; because you would acquire in civilization and the arts, during one hundred years, far more from our teachings than you could gain by a too rapid departure from our shores.

Yet, after all that has been said of the glory you would acquire in assuming a national character, and redeeming your own land from depravity, the fact that at least three generations must pass away before a striking and lasting effect can be produced upon all your native brethren who would be brought within your influence, together with the unknown trials that wait upon new settlements, and the comforts, such as they are, which you enjoy here, may tempt you to shrink from your real duty. I have endeavoured to define and enforce it by the most solid arguments; and, before you do decide against this advice, let me once more entreat you to take your present condition into solemn consideration. Then, if your are convinced, as I think you must be, that you really possess the power to be of service to Africa, do not be deterred from examining the condition of your fatherland, closely and carefully.

If you find your native brethren powerless for the defence of your nation, as were the Indians of this country when we landed on these shores, then let not their weakness turn you from them, but rather suffer it to draw you closer to them. And do not delay the commencement of your work of charity and glory. Remember that the ground you stand upon was depopulated by our sires, without mercy to the original owners. The motives that actuated England *then*, are now as strong as ever. England has recently found her way into the interior of Africa, and it is said that she is even now building steamboats to navigate African rivers. Let us suppose that she should find fertile cotton regions there. These would be of more value to her than her Australian gold mines. With such a treasure in view, she would colonize. If she did not virtually enslave your people, she would seek her profit at the cost of your brethren as unscrupulously and as sternly as she now cultivates opium at the cost of the Hindoo. In such a case, your power for the formation of free states would be seriously limited, as long as African labour could render these cotton fields of value to the English manufacturer. Let us suppose rich gold mines to be discovered in the interior of Africa. Can you think for a moment that the white man would be kept from taking possession of them, were Africa possessed of no other means of resistance than such as your native brethren could offer? Such discoveries are not improbable; and, in the event of either gold mines or cotton fields, or both, being discovered, even Liberia — the scion of civilization and liberty, engrafted upon an African stem — might wither and die! All Africa might be brought under colonial vassalage to the white race. Your chance of establishing a nationality of your own might then be forever lost; or, if Liberia should still be saved for a time by the treaties she has already formed with European nations, her territory would remain too narrow for power, and too feeble for respect. Take your ground, and determine at once that you will live or die for your country! Secure the organization of three or four free states, and you will not only be enabled to defend against all intrusion of the white man a country larger than ours, but you will also secure all that which is valuable in Africa — her spices, her cotton, her coffee, her gold, her unbounded resources of commerce and agriculture. Such advantages will not only assure you of a personal independence, but you will be, like other men, treading this earth their equals, however proud and boastful they may be of their national power and national glory! Your liberty will be complete for your own good. Your example and influence will spread Christianity and freedom throughout the vast multitudes swarming between Abyssinia and the Atlantic, Zahara and the Cape. Your commerce will spread its wings over the Red Sea, the Persian Gulf, and the Indian Ocean, and your influence may even react upon civilization, and check the distinction of races in the Islands of the far-off Pacific.

But even long before these grand results can be accomplished, your energies will have rendered you happy, free, and independent. You will not be as you are here, reduced almost to a single occupation, — that of carrying the hod or working in the field. Your free will in your own land will give you a choice of occupation. You will be your own generals, and your own statesmen; your own lawyers, and your own judges: you will be the laymen, and will choose your own preachers: you will cultivate your own land, and sell the surplus product of your labour: you will build your own ships, and you alone will navigate them: you will work and fatten your own oxen, and you will eat of the fat of the land: you will eat the African deer, instead of the American opossum: you will build your own houses and live in them: you will no longer be obliged to temper the mortar for your "bricks, without straw:" you will be your own tanners and your own shoemakers: in short, when the inclemency of the weather confines you to your houses, your indoor occupations will keep you from starving. Such are the blessings within reach of your own hands, if you will but exert your energies to seize them. And what are your chances for happiness, good and comfortable living, and independence here? I say — *none!* But you say that your hopes rest with the efforts which the Abolitionists are making for you!

Attributes which dignify man; such as honour, virtue, and patriotism; are judged of arbitrarily, according to the prejudices and peculiar social position of the judge: they are terms applied *indefinitely* by society. Men, in their daily walks, are estimated, not by their real motives, but by what they do, and still more by what they leave undone; and when the scrutiny is not made with unusual wisdom, they may receive credit for the practice of the highest virtues, even when their conduct is dictated by selfishness, baseness, vice, and treason. Now, you may consent to erect the proper standard for your duty in relation to African independence and Christian civilization, yet, for want of proper care and attention on your part, you may fail to come up to that standard; and, in that case, you will be judged by the whole world for your actual omission of duty, however good may be your intentions. Let me ask you to examine your supposed or avowed friends by this same rule, lest you attribute to them a degree of virtue or wisdom of which either their real intentions, or their sins of omission may render them entirely unworthy. This is necessary, even to your own defence.

Your relations with us, as strangers in a foreign land; the bondage of your brethren; your own serfdom; your present condition and your future prospects; all these things are *positive facts*, and can be judged of accordingly. You should endeavour to judge of the value of your friends, not by their professions in advocating what is "right," but by the bearing of their actual conduct on these evils of which you so justly complain. Hence; when the Abolitionist proclaims upon *his* standard, *equal rights in citizenship and labour*, for the elevation of your race to social equality in this country, and appeals to *humanity* in defence of those rights, it is a duty and even a necessity for you to inquire into his *acts*, and examine whether his *practices* come up to the requirements of this standard. If, for example, he maintains that the country is large enough for you and us, and that there is labour enough for us all, it will be proper for you, before you place implicit confidence in his assertions, to ascertain whether he is really active in seeking, for your benefit, a proper distribution of labour, in such a way as to make his professions of use to you; whether he is seeking places for your sons in machine shops, carpenter shops, and stores, and in this way endeavouring to secure all manner of trades for your children. If you find that he is not doing so, then you must perceive at once that the vast extent of country we possess, and the vast amount of labour we have to perform, will have no other effect upon *you* than to aggravate the positive evils you now endure, in consequence of the want of proper employment during inclement weather. Now, there are hundreds of you who are capable of entering into this inquiry — hundreds who must fully understand that, with the increase of your population, the evils of the want of a proper distribution of labour in your behalf will increase upon you; especially as your experience teaches you, even now, that the amount of your outdoor labour becomes daily more limited by the rapid increase of *our race*. Thus you must see that misery upon misery must accumulate upon you in the future, and that that which is scarcely bearable now, will become intolerable when you number twenty millions in a foreign land. This must be so; for we can measure the depths of degradation, vice, and treason which may depress a people, but we can never measure the height to which honour, virtue, and patriotism can elevate it.

For your encouragement, stores are established where nothing but the product of free labour is sold, and it is strongly urged by some of your friends that England should seek new cotton fields, to enable her to refuse to purchase the product of slave labour, in order to compel the master to liberate the slave, by destroying the value of his labour. This is like many other projects for your benefit—wholly ineffective! But if it could really be carried into effect, it would prove terribly prejudicial to your brethren, the slaves. The idea of starving the master without also starving the slave, is preposterous. That which seriously affects the one, must of necessity, and in like manner, affect the other, besides probably leading to insurrection. This irrational measure would seriously affect the monetary concerns of the whole country. The policy, in itself, is full of mischief, without having the power to accomplish for your race the least possible good. The result of such an experiment upon a large scale, would prove surely productive of wide-spread suffering and misery to your race.

Now, your friends urge the plausible plea that the division of labour is "*your right*," and that nothing but prejudice can prevent you from the enjoyment of this right. But when they, as well as you, know that they do not exert themselves to secure this right, and have neither hope nor power to remove this prejudice, their pretensions can have no other effect than to encourage agitation, and disturb the harmony of the Union, while inducing society, at the same time, to regard *you* as the real cause of all its troubles.

In the perverted use which the Abolitionist makes of the plea of equal rights for you, I think I can show that all their exertions in your behalf are in a great measure neutralized by their own action.

The declaration of " equal rights " engrafted upon our institutions, has no legal meaning or intention, except as applicable to the citizens of the United States; yet your Abolition friends would make this declaration apply to you, and the whole world besides. They not only contend that every foreigner who comes here, although he never had a right to a vote in the country from which he came, has that right *naturally* here, but that it is wrong to deprive him of his vote for the shortest possible time; that it is wrong to prevent the foreigner from taking land; that he has a natural right to it; and, in this way, they pervert the whole meaning of this human law, because, in the abstract, their view is "right" by a "higher law." But in contending for this as broadly as they do, let us inquire how it affects the hopes by which they flatter you into a belief of their friendship. The immigration from Europe into this country for the last few years, has reached the rate of à thousand for each day in the year, or nearly so. The majority of these men have never seen men of your colour, until they arrive upon our shores; a majority of them are poor like yourselves. The first thing many of them aim at is *labour;* in seeking which they are aided by societies formed for the purpose, among whom the humane Abolitionist perhaps may also be found. Labour is secured for them, at your expense. As it so happens that you, as labourers, stand directly in the way of their expectations, they at once take a dislike to you; and you know that a large portion of them hold absolute antipathies against you of the strongest kind, and are not disposed to show you any quarter. Yet these are the men that are encouraged *by your friends* to come up regularly to the ballot-box in due course of time; so that they are obliged to ask of your worst enemies the right of admitting you to vote, because it is "right!" This appears to *me*, however it may seem to *you*, very much like asking a man to come out of a room where he is nearly suffocated with smoke, whilst taking care to have the door secured by a secret enemy.

If the Abolitionist would do *his own voting* until you could be brought upon the same platform with the foreigner, you might have some hope; but as long as the foreigner has a vote *and you none* — he having no regard for you, not even from habitual acquaintance—you can have no hopes of citizenship in this country. For your own benefit, too many guests are invited; the loaf is cut and divided before it reaches the second table. So that, even the fact that "all men are born equal," and have "equal rights," is of no use to you *here*, you not being citizens; nor is it of any avail to your friends for your benefit, but serves their purpose merely for agitation, with a view to their own. Your peculiar relation to this country ought to render you extremely doubtful of any proffered favours, unless you can clearly understand that these favours are predicated upon a practical basis. Let me conjure you, then, while you are yet few in numbers, whilst Africa stands open to receive you, and whilst means are being made ready for your transit, to remain no longer (I will not say traitors) indifferent to your country: for there is a possibility, if you should remain here until your population becomes so vast, and your burdens so much increased, as to cause you to cry aloud for relief in the midst of your sufferings, as did the Children of Israel, that the door of African hospitality may be closed against you. New developments of Africa are daily being made, and it is impossible to tell what those developments may bring forth.

The institutions of society are of the sternest character. Yes! even `a Christian civilization has no sympathy for a neglect or omission of duties. Charity appeals for mercy, but, alas! too often in vain. Society appreciates individuals only for their worth, because worthy men alone constitute good society. Hence; even the profligate, the vicious, and the idle of the white race are sufferers, even now, as much as yourselves.

That which I wish you to understand fully is, not only your individual connection and partial dependence upon us, but your relation, as a nation, to society at large and the brotherhood of men. When you do understand the all-important truths in relation to your condition, which I have so frankly urged upon your attention, you will not regard the unmeaning appeals of demagogues, and kind-hearted but misguided theorists, for your elevation here; but you will work and act like men to secure your elevation in your own country. You are perfectly familiar with the fact that the society of Europe, governed by a Christian civilization, seized upon this country, and removed from its path of progress the native and original proprietor. Whatever the mysterious designs of the all-wise Ruler of the Universe may have been, in permitting this seemingly dark deed to be done, the facts which have so strikingly facilitated the event are these: — The natives depended solely upon the bounties of nature; and, rather than work, they continually reduced their numbers within the means of living upon a providential supply, by warring upon each other. Their removal made way for an industrious race upon the same ground—a race with flourishing fields; a race augmenting the means of subsistence and comfort in more than a hundred-fold, by the proper exercise of that intellect which God himself breathed into the nostrils of our first progenitor; and thus, by the development of the hidden treasures of the earth for the comforts of man and the glory of God himself, millions upon millions of human beings are now made the recipients of an earthly happiness and a hope of Heaven, which, under the rule of savage tribes and savage customs, would never have existed. But was this "right?" Here is a theme for the divine and the philosopher! If properly inquired into and explained, it may show how much good may sometimes grow out of evil. But, for our purpose, the reference to the fact itself is sufficient.

You see your own nation idle and degraded, and entirely unmindful of the duty it owes to itself and the God you worship; you see society and Christian civilization progressing with the same sternness now that characterized its march three hundred years ago, —demanding the active exercise of the high duties which each man owes to his neighbour and to his God, and still proclaiming honour to the man who will make two spears of grass grow where but one grew before! And, as your knowledge of the fact that God has permitted one idle and degraded nation to be removed from the face of the earth is so complete, what right have you to believe that He will not permit the removal of another for like causes? Should such be the fate of your fatherland in the rapid progress of the white race, then, when you shall number millions in this land, will the dark side of the picture of your destiny be brought into view indeed!

We can have no reason to entertain, for one moment, the belief that God will desert those who are dutiful in obeying his will. Let us then suppose that the aborigines of America had numbered 500,000 of their race in Europe, previous to the European colonization of this country. Let us suppose that they had, then and there, possessed the same knowledge of freedom and the Christian religion which you now enjoy; that they had brought their knowledge with them to this land, as they might then have done; that they had established here free states, and enlightened their brethren; do you not believe that, instead of leaving to us all the blessings this country affords us, and will continue to afford to millions of our race, *they* would now be in the fruition of all these enjoyments themselves? I do! Let us suppose, however, that these 500,000 American Indians in Europe had refused to be instrumental in the redemption of their native land, and rather chose to remain servants in Europe. What, in this case, should we now think of their blindness?

With these friendly remarks I leave you, in the hope that your race will profit by them, through all future time.

CONCLUSION.

I THOUGHT I had finished, but I must hold you a little longer.

While these pages have been passing through the press, a new territorial Government has been organized by Congress. The "act" for this purpose has almost monopolized the attention of the national legislature at the present session; and all that gave the measure special interest in discussion, and that will constitute its importance in application, is its bearing upon *slavery* and the *public lands!*

Thus you see I have not busied myself upon a far-fetched or subordinate subject. It is one that forces itself upon our attention in every speech at Washington, and in every newspaper throughout the Republic. It has awakened an unquiet spirit that defies exorcism either by the patriot or the wily politician. And I am glad it does so!

I have dedicated this volume to the Congress of the United States. It was proper for me to do so. But I was aware from the first, my countrymen, that my final and prevailing appeal must be made to you. The lust of power and the coils of patronage will restrain the strongest sinews. You are yet Samsons unbound: listen, then, as to a great deliverance from a great danger; for the evil has already come home to our hearths and our bosoms.

No portion of the human family has ever borne such a relation to the whole, as our nation does to the rest of the world at this time. We hold civil liberty for our own happiness, but also in trust for all mankind; and as we demean ourselves under its influence, so will the great cause be advanced or retarded. "Can a man take fire into his bosom and not be burned?" And can men trample upon the essentials of liberty, and yet enjoy its life and strength? Certainly not. Then believe me, that *our* action on the disposition of the Public Domain, and upon the institution of slavery, will determine the question of peace or strife for our own generation, and stamp the inheritance of our successors for good or evil. If we suffer the public lands to be grasped by a few demagogues, we shall create a landed aristocracy. If we give these lands away to the vagabond and adventurer, we shall be squandering the means of the world's independence. And, if we foster and extend slavery, we shall be found enacting feudalism on the soil hitherto consecrated by the Declaration of Independence.

> "Can such things be,
> And overcome us like a summer cloud,
> Without our special wonder?"

Let no one persuade you that this is mere declamation: it is stern truth, which we may now see and soon shall feel.

Our grand preliminary measure is a change of custody for the Public Domain. I propose that we create a special authority for that purpose; and I wish this new feature in our great experiment of liberty and law to be accomplished with all due form and order. Its most appropriate commencement will be in an act of Congress authorizing the election of delegates to compose a Convention which shall determine the particulars of a plan of operation. But — Congress may refuse to do this!

It is in view of this contingency that I have turned back to you with these "few more last words."

Should Congress not authorize this Convention; should your representatives refuse this righteous request; then must every township call its primitive meeting, and, like the "Caulkers' Club" in Boston of old, take this matter up as individuals, and agitate, and resolve, and *vote*, until this great measure be accomplished.

THE END.